T 8570   *21021*

DATE DUE

AUG. O 4 2003			
OCT. 1 7 2005			
DEC. O 4 2006			

Coping with

BIPOLAR DISORDER AND MANIC-DEPRESSIVE ILLNESS

Joann Jovinelly

The Rosen Publishing Group, Inc.
New York

To my mother, Anna, and my late father, Joseph, who both taught me to strive for my very best, every day

Published in 2001 by The Rosen Publishing Group, Inc.
29 East 21st Street, New York, NY 10010

Cover photo © Craig Witkowski/Indexstock

Library of Congress Cataloging-in-Publication Data

Jovinelly, Joann.
Coping with bipolar disorder and manic-depressive illness / by Joann Jovinelly.
p. cm. — (Coping)
Includes bibliographical references and index.
ISBN 0-8239-3193-5
1. Manic-depressive illness—Juvenile literature. 2. Manic-depressive illness in adolescence—Juvenile literature. [1. Manic-depressive illness. 2. Mental illness.] I. Title. II. Series.
RC516 .J684 2001
616.89'5—dc21

2001001311

Manufactured in the United States of America

Contents

Introduction   1

1   Recognizing Mental Illness   5

2   Mania   16

3   Depression   28

4   Bipolar Disorder   37

5   Seeking Professional Help   48

6   The Advent of Modern Drug Therapies:

Mood Stabilizers   55

7   Antidepressants, Antipsychotics,

and Other Treatments   64

8   Living with Bipolar Disorder   78

Glossary   84

Where to Go for Help   86

For Further Reading   88

Index   89

Introduction

> The beauty of the world has two edges, one of laughter and one of anguish.
>
> —Virginia Woolf, A Room of One's Own

Rachael

Bipolar disorder forces you to appreciate your life. After suffering from a period of severe depression, I am thankful to be alive. I have experienced both extremes—severe mania and severe depression—many times. I have walked on the edge and have come back. I feel that my emotions are more expansive than those of others who have never experienced such states of mood and emotion. Sure, some people get depressed . . . but true depression is like death itself. Experiencing bipolar depression is like dying, both mentally and physically, and then bouncing back to reality. It gives you insight into living.

Thankfully, I have channeled my manic thoughts and episodes into my artistic career, working with graphics and photography. I have the focus and insight to create beautiful pieces that are greatly admired. The mental health of many famous artists has been unstable, and many of them may have been afflicted with bipolar disorder. Even former president Abraham Lincoln was believed to have been bipolar; so are modern-day celebrities like Robin Williams and Carrie Fisher.

A Complex Disorder

Precisely defining and diagnosing any mental illness is a challenge for both doctor and patient. This is especially

1

true when isolating instances of bipolar disorder, simply because it exhibits a variety of symptoms that, at a glance, may or may not be related. Although most people are familiar with the symptoms associated with clinical depression (unipolar depression) most are uncertain about the distinction between this state of mind and the depressive symptoms associated with manic depression, today most commonly referred to as bipolar disorder.

The depression that is felt by individuals with bipolar disorder is not a constant depression. Bipolar depression is less clearly delineated by feeling hopeless or helpless. It also has the potential to combine depressive feelings with irritability, aggression, hostility, or increased activity.

First and foremost, bipolar disorder is a mood disorder of the brain. This emotional disorder is termed "bi," meaning two, because it fluctuates generally between two active states, or "polar" opposites of mood—from feeling severe sadness or depression to feeling elated, happy, overly enthusiastic, or manic. These mood changes tend to occur in cycles, sometimes slowly or sometimes rapidly, depending on the type of bipolar disorder. What distinguishes the mood swings of bipolar disorder from mood changes felt by most people is the extreme nature and intensity of the emotions.

Also, the mood changes often follow a pattern. This characteristic of a recurrent pattern in emotional mood changes is distinctive. It enables doctors to more accurately distinguish bipolar disorder from other, more familiar mental disturbances, such as clinical depression.

Because it is an emotional disorder, bipolar disorder influences a person's ability to regulate his or her own mood or level of emotion. The body's hormone levels and natural chemicals regulate functions such as blood pressure and body temperature; they also help control emotions. A bipolar person tends to have more difficulty regulating his or her emotions. He or she feels very happy, elated, or manic, and then feels severely saddened or depressed.

Chances are that you have heard people say they are "manic," "depressed," or even "psychotic," in casual conversation. Although these terms may vividly describe mood changes, chances are that they are an exaggeration. Most individuals never suffer from psychosis, a mental condition in which the ability to gauge reality is seriously impaired. Some people do suffer from bouts of true depression or mania.

The difference between what some may describe casually as depression or mania, and the clinical states of manic-depression lies in the severity of the illness itself, its symptoms, and its duration. The severity of a person's encounters with both depression and mania result from that person's specific biology, his or her environment, and his or her genetic composition. Some doctors believe that although most people have slight mood swings (especially teenagers who are experiencing many hormonal changes), only those individuals with a genetic predisposition to bipolar disorder actually suffer the severe mood swings that are discussed in this book.

Bipolar disorder, the illness that causes symptoms of depression and mania, can only be diagnosed by a mental health professional such as a psychiatrist or psychologist. Unfortunately, an illness like bipolar disorder is highly complex and evasive; its diagnosis often eludes patients and doctors alike. The reason for this is simple: Bipolar disorder wears many faces. It is a biological mood disorder as individual as the mind itself.

Other factors that contribute to the mystifying nature of this condition are its ability to hide and then resurface for no apparent reason. Physicians call bipolar disorder a "relapsing and remitting" illness simply because its symptoms come and go, an attribute of all mood-related disorders. In some cases, bipolar disorder is difficult to diagnose, treat, and study. Because of this, most individuals suffering from this malady spend years searching for effective treatments. Many reach a conclusive diagnosis only after seeing more than three doctors.

This is not to say that there are no options for individuals coping with this and other mood disorders. Currently, there are more methods of treatment available than ever before, including proven drug therapies such as lithium, experimental homeopathic treatments, and new research that points to the increased value of altered diet and exercise programs. Although bipolar disorder may present a complicated twist of actions and reactions to both doctor and patient, it is now considered a manageable illness.

Bipolar disorder does not discriminate. Currently, there are an estimated 2.2 million people suffering from this dynamic and changeable mental illness in the United States alone. Many others remain undiagnosed. Unfortunately, many individuals do not seek treatment for many years. The National Depressive and Manic-Depressive Association estimates that more than 36 percent of those suffering from bipolar disorder remain undiagnosed.

The keys to unlocking the secrets of bipolar disorder are education and research. In just one decade, doctors have been able to explain and isolate important information about factors surrounding this disease. More and more, researchers are uncovering the vast complexities of the brain. Learning about bipolar disorder is just one path to discovery.

Recognizing Mental Illness

The history of melancholia includes all of us.
—Henry Charles Bukowski

Long before physicians developed the terms "bipolar disorder" and "manic-depression," the illness was widely written about. Even as far back as the second century AD, a philosopher named Areteus discussed groups of individuals who would "laugh, play, dance night and day, and sometimes go openly to the crowded market, as if victors in some contest of skill." He then described how these same individuals later appeared "torpid, dull, and sorrowful."

The Ancients

In the fifth century AD, the scholar Hippocrates wrote of a mystifying sense of sadness categorized by its "restless nature, despondency, sleeplessness, irritability and lack of appetite." His observation, "Grief and fear, when lingering, provoke melancholia," is just as relevant today as it was in ancient times. Back then, physicians attributed illness to a person's character and makeup, or what they called the body's balance of fluids, or "humors." The study was known as humoralism. Melancholia was synonymous with madness and was actually derived from the Greek word for black bile. As you may already know, melancholia is now a word often used to describe depression.

By the second century AD, the Romans had formulated what they considered a comprehensive humoral theory, dividing humanity into four different body types: blood bile, yellow bile, phlegm, and black bile. Personality was thought to be one of four types: choleric, phlegmatic, sanguine, or melancholic. For example, if a person was thought to be warm in nature, giving, happy, and outgoing, his or her body type was formed from excess blood bile and his or her personality type was sanguine.

Depression, it was believed, resulted from an imbalance in humors. The Roman physician Galen argued that black bile "darkened the seat of reason." Similar to our own modern theories of genetics, a person who consisted wholly of this black bile was thought to have a predisposition for melancholia or depression. Nightmares, the Romans believed, were brought on by a sudden flow of black bile into the brain. The ancients also linked depression and euphoria. A manic temperament resulted from an excess of yellow bile. The humoral theory for mania was that the dominating yellow bile fluids actually burned within the body, turned black, and then caused depressive tendencies.

As time passed, however, heated debate raged as to whether depression stemmed from a genetic source and was passed down from mother or father to child or whether it was an illness that could develop on its own. We now know that genetics plays a huge role in the development of any mental illness, including bipolar disorder.

6

Depression and Religion

Religious interpretations of manic-depression remained popular for centuries. The philosopher Plato believed that some depression was mystical in nature; ancient philosophers often equated madness with divinity. Madness, or "divine inspiration," was commonly linked with communication with the gods. Socrates himself wrote, "madness comes from God, whereas sober sense is merely human."

Religious beliefs helped inform not only the definition of manic-depression but also the method of treatment. After the collapse of the Roman Empire, the overall treatment of manic-depressives became much less humane. It was then believed that individuals stricken with bouts of expressive mania were channeling voices from the devil. Authorities placed patients in chains to restrict them from communicating with others. Further treatments included bloodletting, applying electric eels to the skull of the afflicted, administering exotic herbal potions, and finally, in the most extreme cases, performing euthanasia.

Early Christians were convinced of a depressive's divine connections. At this point in Western civilization, the mentally ill were seen as the responsibility of the clerics, humoral theories were discounted, and any mental disorder was thought of as a sin against the church. Later, these same ideas would further intermingle with celestial notions that characterized mental disturbances as occurring largely at night, inspired by the Moon. This reveals the origin of the term "lunatic," meaning that the presence of the moon (*luna*) inspires someone to become deranged.

These ideas persisted unabated until the sixteenth century, when physicians began to research other causes of depression. The first mental hospitals were also established at this time. Unfortunately, these facilities often treated patients cruelly. Michael H. Stone, M.D. contends in *Healing the Mind: A History of Psychiatry from Antiquity to the Present,* that there may be a link between mania and witch trials conducted in 1692, in Salem, Massachussetts. During the trials, some physicians testified that the seemingly suspicious behavior of women accused of being witches actually resulted from medical conditions such as hysteria or mania.

Manic-Depression

In the eighteenth century, during the age of the Enlightenment, however, physicians had returned to investigating the link between depression and mania. Earlier, in 1686, a doctor named Theophile Bonet began using a term he'd coined to indicate the connection between mania and melancholia: manico-melancolicus. Bonet's theory was echoed in the eighteenth century by an English physician named Robert James, who wrote, "We find that melancholic patients easily fall into madness, which, when removed, the melancholy again discovers itself."

The first published theories that conclusively coupled mania and depression, however, were delivered to a nineteenth-century French scientific journal nearly simultaneously by two doctors. The first documentation came from Jules Baillarger in 1854, followed two weeks later by Jean-Pierre Falret. Each wrote comprehensive articles outlining similar theories about manic-depression. They described it as a mental illness that fluctuated between mania and sadness and that was interrupted periodically by periods of normal moods and behaviors.

Later in the nineteenth century, Karl Ludwig Kahlbaum became the first scientist to recognize manic-depression as a unique disorder. While observing what he termed "abnormal behaviors" in depressed individuals, he wrote of a "cyclic insanity." He also coined the term "cyclothymia." German psychologists remained at the forefront of diagnosing manic-depression for decades. Both Sigmund Freud and Emil Kraeplin strongly suggested a correlation between depression and heredity.

Kraeplin, who was ultimately responsible for distinguishing manic-depression from other mental disorders, wrote about it extensively in his *Textbook of Psychiatry*— a text still heralded today. In 1899, he argued that "all mental illness is connected," a revolutionary idea at the time that is now widely accepted by modern scientists and doctors. By 1904, his suggested remedies for periods of mania included long hot water baths, bed rest, less socialization with others, and a medicinal solution consisting primarily of bromide of sodium.

By the 1950s, though, treatments for manic-depression became much more aggressive. Severely manic patients were hospitalized and routinely isolated. The administration of drugs, including barbiturates and narcotics, was also common. Sometimes the preferred method of treatment was continued sedation. Other, nondrug treatments included shock therapies, electrical induction, and surgical prefrontal lobotomy. Except for electroconvulsive therapies, these treatments were discontinued a decade after the discovery of antipsychotic drugs, like chlorpromazine, also known as Thorazine.

This drug has a specific effect on psychotic symptoms and was the beginning of a revolution in drug therapy.

Freudian psychoanalysis and treatment dominated studies of depression until the 1970s. Interestingly, Freud himself believed that eventually, all mental illness would be treated with chemical drug therapies. In fact, today we tend to view mental illness in a more biological light. Currently, most scientists and lay people believe that depression results from a combination of genetic susceptibility and environmental factors, both of which cause biological changes in the brain. However, this explanation does not totally discount the ancients and their elaborate explanations of people's emotional disposition. In many ways, their theories were insightful and were far ahead of their time.

The Expression of Depression

Historically, many hundreds of creative personalities have suffered with what we now call bipolar disorder. Anguished poetry, paintings, and narratives testify to the timelessness of mood disorders and mental illness itself. Kay Redfield Jamison, Ph.D., professor of psychiatry at the Johns Hopkins School of Medicine and accomplished author, is an expert on mood disorders and mental illness. Jamison hypothesizes a connection between the nature of bipolar disorder and the creative mind in *Touched With Fire: Manic-Depressive Illness and the Artistic Temperament*. She eloquently describes how creative forces rumble within episodes of mania. Jamison explores the connection between manic-depression and the works of luminaries such as painters Vincent van Gogh, Jackson Pollack, and Mark Rothko;

writers Virginia Woolf, Hermann Hesse, and Edgar Allan Poe; and poets Emily Dickinson, T. S. Eliot, Sylvia Plath, and Theodore Roethke. Jamison wrote about her own intimate struggles with bipolar disorder, too, after being diagnosed with the disease in her mid-twenties, in her memoir, *An Unquiet Mind.*

The marriage of creativity and manic-depression, she argues, is no accident, for the same passion that plunges people into the darkest depths of despair is also the energy that fuels their moments of artistic genius. For years, scholars and educators alike recalled Edgar Allan Poe's manic temperament, his nights of lunacy slowed or stilled under the swells of an alcoholic stupor. Moreover, who could forget the haunting and obsessive refrain of the bells, bells, bells in his poem of the same name. Poe was a master poet, with the ability to capture his manic spirit in every line. The fourth stanza of "The Bells," written in 1849, is a further example of Poe's ability to channel his manically fueled emotions.

Hear the tolling of the bells—
Iron Bells!
What a world of solemn thought their monody compels!
In the silence of the night,
How we shiver with affright
At the melancholy menace of their tone!
For every sound that floats
From the rust within their throats
Is a groan.
And the people—ah, the people—
They that dwell up in the steeple,
All Alone
And who, tolling, tolling, tolling,

In that muffled monotone,
Feel a glory in so rolling
On the human heart a stone—
They are neither man nor woman—
They are neither brute nor human—
They are Ghouls:
And their king it is who tolls;
And he rolls, rolls, rolls,
Rolls
A paean from the bells!
And his merry bosom swells
With the paean of the bells!
And he dances, and he yells;
Keeping time, time, time,
In a sort of Runic rhyme,
To the paean of the bells—
Of the bells:
Keeping time, time, time,
In a sort of Runic rhyme,
To the throbbing of the bells—
Of the bells, bells, bells—
To the sobbing of the bells;
Keeping time, time, time,
As he knells, knells, knells,
In a happy Runic rhyme,
To the rolling of the bells—
Of the bells, bells, bells:
To the tolling of the bells,
Of the bells, bells, bells, bells—
Bells, bells, bells—
To the moaning and the groaning of the bells.

Poe was frequently ill at ease, and he often reached out through long, painfully written letters to his friends to ask for help and salvation from his depressive state. Like Poe, many writers have sought solace in alcohol or drugs, hoping to mute the tortures of depression and mania. The lives of so many famous literary figures (and known depressives) were and are hindered by alcoholic tendencies. F. Scott Fitzgerald, Ernest Hemingway, Tennessee Williams, Robert Lowell, and Jack Kerouac have all written about their struggles with substance abuse, depression, and mood swings.

Many people who experience the heavy toll of bipolar disorder understand the misguided attraction to drugs and alcohol. Some physicians also acknowledge that a large percentage of their patients self-medicate with drugs and alcohol. Studies now indicate that many sufferers try to prolong the high-energy manic state of the bipolar cycle by abusing stimulants such as cocaine or even caffeine. Many report that substance-assisted mania is many times more attractive to them than their depressive states.

Others use depressants like alcohol to silence mania's compulsions. According to Kay Redfield Jamison, "excesses of all kinds dominate a manic personality." As reported in an investigation conducted by the National Institute of Mental Health in major cities across the United States, there is evidence of alcoholism and drug abuse among approximately 60 percent of patients diagnosed with manic-depressive illness.

However, research also points out that drug abuse of any sort combined with bipolar mood swings is a recipe for disaster, exaggerating already unstable emotional reactions, or sending bipolar individuals into a state of numbness. There may be an even deeper connection between being afflicted with bipolar disorder and drug and alcohol abuse. Evidence suggests that substance abuse might contribute to the very development of mood disorders. Some research indicates that individuals who are genetically susceptible to substance abuse may also be genetically predisposed to mood disorders. Physicians hypothesize that perhaps these two problems so often occur in tandem because the genes (for addiction and bipolar disorder) are located on the same chromosome and are therefore jointly inherited. Most disturbing, the suicide rate for those considered dual-diagnosis individuals (substance abusers who suffer from a mood disorder) is dramatic. One 1993 study found that 48 percent of those who committed suicide had both a history of substance abuse and a mood disorder.

Mood Disorders

Bipolar disorder (also known as manic-depression) is a mood disorder that has elements of both depression and mania. These vastly different emotional states are sometimes experienced as isolated states, or as complex combinations or mixed states of both depression and mania. Simply put, a bipolar personality exhibits extremes of mood or emotion. These emotions are out of proportion; to others they seem intense and unreasonable. Doctors diagnose mood disorders only after gathering a great deal of information about a person's lifestyle, environment, medical history, and other important facts about his or her personality and emotional responses.

Generally, there are two types of mood disorders: unipolar depressive disorders and bipolar disorders. For the purposes of this book, unipolar mood disorders are mood disorders that consistently depress or flatten a person's mood. Bipolar mood disorders are more complex and have both a depressive and manic tendency.

For people experiencing the effects of bipolar depression, the shift from one emotional state to another is often dramatic. However, because these effects may occur over time, sometimes over many months or even years, they are often dismissed, attributed to life situations, and unfortunately remain undiagnosed. People normally experience the first signs of bipolar disorder in their teens or early twenties. It is sometimes described as a feeling of unsettling desire. The bipolar state of mania is often described as experiencing a sense of endless urgency.

Kate

The first time that I went through a manic period, I thought I was having the time of my life. I loved school and my grades were excellent. I was staying after school, helping with the yearbook and competing on the swim team. A week or so before final exams, I stayed awake for a few nights to cram for the tests. Soon after, I found that I was missing meals, getting more irritable, and feeling an endless stream of uncontrollable thoughts and ideas. I talked a lot. My friends accused me of being self-centered. I was too busy to recognize it then, but my behavior had really changed.

Mania

Bipolar individuals experience stages of both mania and depression. Unlike the lethargic and sad thoughts and emotions felt by a person who is depressed, stages of mania experienced by bipolar individuals can be enthusiastic, energetic, and inspired. These pleasurable emotions develop over time and escalate easily, often into states of total euphoria. For a person's mood to be considered manic, he or she must experience several symptoms of mania for at least one consecutive week. These symptoms are varied and may include an increased level of grandiosity (a feeling of grand splendor or exaggeration), a decreased need for sleep, intense activity, and an excessive need to communicate.

The Manic State

In the manic state, the mood switch is set to "high," as opposed to a depressive "low." Often, a manic state will take weeks, even months, to develop fully, with each passing day becoming more crazed with activity. A person who is experiencing a state of mania feels as though he or she is thinking more clearly than ever before. It feels as if thought processes have been accelerated. Actually, this is not the case at all. Psychiatrists call this feeling a flight of ideas which quite clearly represents one aspect of mania:

Thoughts can occur in a streamline fashion—one after another in an endless rush. These racing thoughts are nearly always characteristic of a manic state, and they help lead psychiatrists to a bipolar diagnosis.

Many bipolar patients refer to these states of mania as "wonderful," or "better than normal." However, it is important to realize that a state of mania is just as dangerous as a state of depression. Also, not every individual who suffers from bipolar disorder will experience manic symptoms; many can go years without ever experiencing a clinically recognized or full-blown manic episode.

Mania is complex, though, and is sometimes categorized as white or black. White mania is clearly punctuated with the classic symptoms: confident exuberance and energy. Contrastingly, black mania refers to a mixed state of mania that swings from irritability and anger to euphoria without missing a beat.

Although the average onset of the first typical manic episode is likely to occur during a person's early twenties, some people report experiencing their first periods of mania as early as adolescence. In others, the first manic episode begins later, well into mid-life. Regardless of age, episodes of mania typically last from several weeks to several months, but they are generally of a shorter duration than their depressive counterparts. (Although, according to current statistics, bipolar adolescents generally experience more frequent manic episodes rather than depressive ones.)

For most individuals with bipolar disorder, episodes of mania are almost immediately followed by depression, but not in all cases. The *Diagnostic and Statistical Manual of Mental Disorders, (DSM-IV)*, reports that for 50 to 60 percent of bipolar patients, manic episodes are followed immediately by depressive episodes. In the remaining cases, each change in mood is buffered by a short period of normalcy in mood, also known as euthymia.

Rapid or pressured speech patterns are also common symptoms of a manic state. There are many other outward expressions of accelerated mental activity, such as frantic letter writing, compulsively creating lists, or evenings of frenzied telephone calls. Sometimes manic individuals will talk nonstop, for hours at a time, and they are usually difficult to interrupt. To some, these speech patterns may seem clever or witty, punctuated by amusing anecdotes, dramatic mannerisms, or singing.

Many bipolar individuals who are experiencing mania try to corral their ideas because these thoughts seem relevant and meaningful. Nearly every thought takes on a special significance. While in a manic state, a person might feel enlightened or divinely chosen. It is also common for these individuals to engage in other extravagant activities, such as spending large sums of money, racking up debilitating credit card debt, and abusing drugs and alcohol.

Michael

I always know when a strong manic period is coming on. It feels good. I can honestly say that when it happens I do everything in my power to convince myself and others that I am okay because I don't want my power and control to end. I seem to have all the right words to say to people; even strangers seem taken with me. I could be in a checkout line and fearlessly strike up conversations with everyone. During times of mania, no one is a stranger. I do not sleep well.

I cannot sleep. I find something to do to occupy my mind while I stay awake. I am very creative during episodes of mania. I feel more confident, and I am more artistically inclined. In those manic moments, I often come up with ideas for my second job as a freelance Web designer. It is as if mania has created an aching in my body, an urge to do more. During these weeks, rest is impossible.

Other characteristics that distinguish the manic state are a decreased need for sleeping and eating. It is common for a person in the throes of mania to go nights without sleep or to skip one meal after another. The results of mania can therefore be very dramatic over time. Other early warning signs of an impending manic state include: any activity done to excess (such as shopping or spending large amounts of money), long periods of excitability, feeling an urgent need to communicate, and feeling a constant sense of distraction.

Symptoms of Mania

The symptoms of mania—"mania" being the Latin word for madness—are extremely varied, and are usually very individualistic. Psychiatrists define mania and manic states according to the level—or stages—of hyperactivity: stage I mania, stage II mania, or stage III mania, also known as dysphoric mania. In addition, there is another, milder type of mania, called hypomania. Still, a manic episode or experience does contain certain common characteristics. Psychiatrists use these features to diagnose mania and differentiate it from hyperactivity or elation. It is also important to understand that a medical professional can more fully observe and interpret the dynamics of a mental disorder. Even if your symptoms seem similar to symptoms common in manic episodes, it is important to consult a qualified professional.

To be diagnosed as manic, one would have to exhibit three or more of the following symptoms for at least one consecutive week. A psychiatrist would also have to consider the effects of outside influences that might con-tribute to the causes of mania, such as complications from medications, electroconvulsive (ECT) or light therapies, abuse of recreational drugs, or another medical condition.

Symptoms of Mania

- Great sudden happiness or euphoria

- Irritability or aggressive behaviors

- Heightened concentration

- Increased energy level or hyperactivity

- Decreased need for sleep or insomnia

- Changes in appetite; eating too much or too little

- Delusional thoughts, or believing false truths

- Hallucinations, or hearing or seeing something that isn't real

- Racing thoughts, or ideas that come one after another

- Rapid speech

- Increased spending

- Distractibility

- Carelessness

- Unwarranted and excessive pleasurable activity

- Use of drugs or alcohol

Frances

I always liked the way my mother explained my manic states to me. She used to compare me to an old-style record player. You remember—the turntables with three speed selections? She said that while the rest of the world ran at 33 rpm, I ran at a speedy 78. It was exactly how I felt at times.

Stage I Mania

To many outsiders, mania appears to be a dramatic performance, a characteristic of an individual's personality. Who, in his or her lifetime has not thought of someone's behavior as crazed, hyperactive, even obsessive? In many instances, these qualities or traits are not simply one's personality. Mania—in the true psychological sense—goes beyond the normal emotional range of feeling. Even stage I mania, clinically classified by medical professionals as the mildest form of mania, can be extreme.

Perhaps the easiest way to think of stage I mania is as an exaggerated version of what might be considered normal thought and activity. While experiencing this "mild mania," a person may feel an expansiveness of thought, his or her speech may become more rapid, or he or she may be more difficult to please. Irritability is a common aspect of this form of mania. A person in an early stage of mania may seem self-centered, overly enthusiastic, even spoiled or demanding of attention and the right to be heard. Others may view his or her behavior—such as speaking to complete strangers, acting rudely, or taking unnecessary risks—as inappropriate. Many bipolar individuals who are familiar with and who can recognize this stage of mania embrace this hyperactivity as a pleasant distraction from sullen or somber periods of depression. In most cases, stage I mania is easily managed and not as debilitating as more advanced manic stages.

Melinda

I can, and still do, spend enormous amounts of money during manic periods. Yet when I am down and depressed—even though I have money—I can barely force myself to pay basic bills. I can identify certain objects in my house that I bought during manic episodes. I can point to them, smile, and associate them with a happier time—a manic time.

Because mania knows no limits, many mental health professionals caution people who suffer with bipolar disorder against using credit cards. I do use three credit cards, but I currently have zero balances. If I start feeling like I'm going to have a bad spree, I hand over my cards and my checkbook to my fiancé to keep from me. It's my safeguard against myself. Spending money for me is like a beer to an alcoholic, a game of cards for a gambler, or a hit of cocaine for a drug addict. I am powerless over it.

Stage II Mania

Stage II mania is an even more accelerated state of mania. It is complex and is sometimes characterized by a tendency to harbor additional emotions (other than euphoric feelings) such as general unpleasantness and depression. Many times a person will swing from an intense period of happiness or satisfaction to periods of anger and frustration.

Irritability at this stage is often expressed openly. Individuals experiencing stage II mania are usually combative, insulting, and disagreeable. It is in this second stage of mania, or mixed mania (as it is sometimes called, because it harbors both manic and depressive tendencies) that a person's racing thoughts or pressured speech tend to become increasingly disorganized. Any preoccupations with obsessive thoughts or actions may become less coherent and even more intense. It is not uncommon for second-stage manic individuals to become delusional, or to believe in false truths.

Delusions begin innocently enough—the person believes that he or she has encountered some great truth or epiphany. Many times, however, individuals who are in the throes of stage II mania exercise poor judgement, believing that they should act on their delusions. Other times, the individuals may find that these delusions dominate their minds. They may feel surrounded or threatened.

Possible delusions include an increased preoccupation with sickness and death or believing very strongly that you are specially chosen for a particular course of events. An individual may also experience what psychiatrists classify as paranoid delusions—the certain belief that his or her life is in imminent danger posed by a specific threat. These moments dog a person from one act to the next, making the person feel as though everyone is out to get him or her. Many people who experience mania of this sort are also preoccupied with religion, and they often feel as though they are being persecuted. Sypmtoms of stage II mania may also include generously doling out advice on matters of which you have no real experience or knowledge, not being able to recognize the need for treatment, and distorting and misinterpreting the true meaning of conversations and comments.

Steve

Mania is like a roller coaster; you go up and you go down but you are screaming inside of your head most of the time. Feelings and thoughts rush through you so quickly that you feel like you can do anything. You feel as if you could rule the world and everyone in it. At least, that's how I felt when I was going through a manic episode.

Mania makes you feel like you are the most powerful person in the room all the time. Whenever I feel this way, I tend to take on too many projects, want to help everyone, and basically spread my resources too thin. I thought what I was feeling was true happiness. I wanted my happiness to contribute to everything that I touched. Looking back, I remember times that I stayed awake for nights on end, making lists, sorting through papers, filing and organizing, until I realized what was happening: I was experiencing an episode of mania.

Stage III Mania

Stage III mania, or dysphoric mania, is very serious, characterized by intensely frenzied and bizarre activity.

24

Psychiatrists use the term dysphoric to describe an increased tenseness of mood or irritability. Incoherent and racing thoughts produce delusions and hallucinations— illusions of seeing, hearing, or sensing things that do not really exist—in nearly one-third of people who experience mania at this advanced stage. Generally, though, auditory hallucinations are far more common than visual ones. In most cases of dysphoric mania, a person is either panic-stricken or in a hopeless state of being. Few individuals experience stage III mania, but for those who do, hospital-ization may be necessary.

In the most extreme cases, people exhibit symptoms of delirious or psychotic mania, an emotional state so extreme that thoughts are almost completely abstracted, seemingly random and incoherent. In addition to being inundated with racing thoughts and extraordinary hallu-cinations, a person in this state is usually very confused and disoriented. He or she may not even know or under-stand the time of day or where he or she resides. He or she may exhibit signs of extreme hostility and paranoia, sometimes destroying his or her personal property or assaulting others. Fortunately, few bipolar patients ever experience stage III mania. For some, in fact, full-blown manic symptoms may never appear at all. Most people with bipolar disorder experience a much more mild form of mania, called hypomania.

Hypomania

What characterizes the hypomanic individual? Simply put, he or she is creative, friendly, intelligent, exciting, and seemingly more alive than many of us. He or she is the person you know as charismatic and witty, someone who would never bat an eye at the thought of an all-night conversation. In short, the hypomanic personality can be quite attractive; people are drawn to it.

A German psychiatrist named Emanuel Mendel coined the term "hypomania" in 1881. He described hypomania as "similar to typical mania, but with a lesser grade of development," (the prefix "hypo" means "under"). Although this state of euphoria has the potential to develop into full-blown mania, according to the *DSM-IV*, less than 15 percent of people who experience hypomania develop full-blown mania. However, it is also possible to suffer from both types of episodes. Although they produce similar symptoms, the degree and severity of those symptoms helps psychiatrists distinguish between these two states. Hypomanic states are never severe enough to warrant hospitalization, however, and they rarely impair a person's social functioning. Symptoms of hypomania are similar to stage I mania. Thoughts and feelings that occupy a person who is feeling the effects of hypomania are accelerated but not disorganized.

Although this state of hyperactivity is never seen as a truly clinical manic state, it has the potential to cause individuals to overestimate their experiences, their intelligence, and their abilities, and may even influence them to reach beyond their means. It is easy to understand this overestimation. Consider the student who refuses to study because he or she is certain of being smart enough to pass the test, or the investor who places all of his or her money in a supposedly sure thing. Many young people who experience hypomanic episodes are frequently absent from school, are substance abusers, are noted for being antisocial, and are poor academic achievers. People struggling with this lesser form of mania may be seduced by its delights, feeling more attractive, more confident, and more self-assured. As a result, they may never seek treatment.

Hypomanic episodes, just like manic and depressive episodes, may be successfully treated with medications. However, because hypomanic symptoms are far less severe than those of mania, many individuals chose to forgo treatment. *This can be an extremely dangerous choice.* In some cases, hypomanic episodes may continue to evolve for years, ruining one's relationships, employment history, or financial status—ultimately, destroying lives. Moreover, because many individuals do not recognize their own hyperactivity or aggressive behavior, they do not realize it is the source of their problems. Instead, these individuals might speak of problems with addiction or of obsessive-compulsive behavioral problems.

Carol

I never knew that I was suffering from a disease that I now recognize as bipolar disorder. Before I was diagnosed, I swung rapidly between states of urgency and despondency. I thought of myself as an "extreme personality." The ups and down in my life never stood out as recurrent patterns until after I began to see a psychiatrist. Now that I'm taking mood-stabilizing medication, I can see the difference between a normal mood and feeling out of control.

Depression

Phillip

I can honestly say I am thankful I have bipolar disorder. The disease runs in my family; both my father and my grandfather suffered from extra-ordinary ups and downs. It sounds really crazy, but I have a greater appreciation for my life. I feel that my feelings run more deeply than they do in other people. I am more sensitive and I feel that I am appreciated because my emotions can run so raw. It's a connecting experience.

The Depressive State

Bipolar disorder is more than a mood disorder flanked by sadness. Although anyone may associate the word "depression" with feelings of despondency, anger, or hopelessness, bipolar depression is unique in that feelings of guilt and shame accompany typical depressive feelings. These guilt-laden emotions are not symptomatic of clinical, unipolar depression and are generally seen as aspects of mood disorders such as bipolar disorder. A person experiencing depression stemming from a mood disorder often feels personally

responsible for that depression. Medical professionals interpret these feelings of guilt as symptoms. These feelings help
them distinguish between those patients with bipolar mood
disorders and those suffering from unipolar depression.

Bipolar depression is very different from what some
people describe as feeling a touch of the blues. Normally,
individuals who may feel a little down in the dumps are
reacting to difficult life experiences such as divorce or
loss of friendships, the trauma of moving to a new home,
or the death of a loved one. Psychiatrists refer to this type
of depression as a reactive depression because it is a
reaction to a situation or environment.

Bipolar depression differs from reactive depression in
that there is no outward reason for its occurrence. It is
commonly described as an overwhelming feeling of sadness, hopelessness, or an awkwardness that is pervasive, in
some instances even an alienation from the body and its
functions. Individuals coping with bipolar depression go
through periods of feeling socially withdrawn, alienated,
or discouraged. Patients report that food has lost its flavor.
Many experience sleepless nights, loss of spirit, thoughts of
suicide and despair, and a sense of their worlds unraveling. Normal symptoms of depression affect nearly every
aspect of a person's existence; depressives often describe a
certain flatness of emotional reaction to everything they
experience. Thinking processes are slowed, as are speech
and movement.

Depressives speak of the loss of enjoyment, or anhedonia. Derived from *hedone,* the Greek word for pleasure,
anhedonia is the inability to feel enjoyment. Many writers,
when putting pen to paper in search of an accurate portrait

of depression, metaphorically link it to suffocation or drowning. Author William Styron describes his battle with the disease in *Darkness Visible,* calling it a "poisonous and leaden mood." Similarly, poet Emily Dickinson described depression as her "hour of lead," while Winston Churchill referred to his moments of despair as "the black dog."

Depression has an uncanny ability to disguise itself in physical ailments, which, over time, can begin to numb a person's sensitivity to his or her general health and well-being. Complaints of constant headaches, stomachaches, nausea, backaches, and fatigue are all potential indicators of depression. Simply dressing for daily activities could make the depressed individual feel a sense of total physical and mental exhaustion. Medical professionals often ask their patients about depression if they complain of symptoms that seemingly have no physical source. Doctors sometimes refer to this type of depression as "masked depression" because patients claim that they do not feel down, or melancholy, but feel unexplainable physical ailments such as backahces.

Decreased energy levels, changes in appetite, insomnia or hypersomnia (sleeping too much), clouded thinking, indecisiveness, and distraction are all standard signs of depression. These changes in thought patterns and a generalized slowing of the mind seem predictable when you consider that they are indeed the opposite symptoms of mania. Many patients have described their worst episodes of depression as a paralysis of the mind. In truth, the brain's cognitive functions slow down during depressive episodes, sometimes to the point where a person is unable to read a book or follow a conversation.

Recurrent irritability, along with angry or suspicious thoughts, is also common. Many patients have reported being plagued by a preoccupation with religion and judgment. It is also not uncommon to find many severely depressed individuals suffering from irrational fears, obsessions, and delusions.

The depressive state is commonly accompanied by thoughts of suicide, homicide, and darkness. Dr. Jamison, who continues her important work of unraveling the nature of manic-depression, talks openly about suicide. She calls suicide an epidemic, noting, "I think that no one has any idea of how many people are dying. Suicide is the second largest killer of women fifteen to forty-four worldwide."

Statistically, suicidal despondency most often occurs in the spring. Interestingly, poet T. S. Eliot, also a depressive, wrote, "April is the cruelest month." Some people contend that after the darkness of winter it is especially difficult for depressives to cope with spring's rebirth. Levels of serotonin, natural chemicals that serve as neurotransmitters, or chemical messengers in the central nervous system, are also lower in winter and early spring. Suicide rates among manic-depressives are among the highest, some 24 percent of those diagnosed, as compared to 1 percent of the general population, according to a study published in the *Archives of General Psychiatry.* Some hypothesize that this high rate of suicide among people struggling with manic-depression is due, in part, to the onset of the depressive state. While in the depressive low of the bipolar cycle, individuals may unfavorably compare themselves to the highly energetic, over-achieving people they were during a manic phase. This may also explain why manic-depressives or individuals diagnosed as bipolar so often fixate on feelings of guilt.

Depressive cycles have also long been associated with seasonal cycles. In fact, some individuals who are diagnosed with bipolar disorder are known as rapid-cyclers because they experience at least four separate episodes of depression, mania, hypomania, or some combination (known as a mixed state) of these mood swings per year. Evidence of a conclusive connection remains unreliable, but historically, manic-depression was nearly always thought of as a distinctive seasonal disorder. Even the Greek scholar Hippocrates noted that mania and melancholia were more likely to occur in the spring and autumn. Although most people report a mood shift during seasonal changes, manic-depressives seem intrinsically more affected by these alterations. In fact, some evidence suggests that they have a higher sensitivity to available light.

Cathy

I feel my bipolar disorder is extremely seasonal. In the spring and summer I am more likely to be manic and rapid-cycling, sleeping only three to five hours per night. In the fall and winter I am much more likely to be depressed and sluggish. I have noticed a pattern of extreme phases every three years. When I am manic, I am very manic. When I am depressed, I am extremely depressed.

Symptoms of Depression

As with mania, doctors categorize depression according to the severity and frequency of its symptoms. It is from a person's description of his or her manic and depressive episodes that medical professionals piece together an initial diagnosis of bipolar disorder. Although this may not be typical of all depressive episodes, statistics show that

50 percent of people who experience an episode of depression will relapse within eighteen months. Of those individuals who have a second episode of depression, 70 percent will very likely experience a third. Finally, 90 percent of individuals who suffer from three episodes of depression will experience related relapses—some for their entire lives.

The symptoms of depression, unlike mania, are consistent. Depressive episodes have characteristics that psychiatrists use to distinguish patients experiencing a depressive low of bipolar disorder. A person would need to exhibit five of the following symptoms for at least two consecutive weeks in order to be diagnosed with depression. A psychiatrist would also have to eliminate the possibility that outside influences caused the depression. As with any diagnosis, however, only a medical professional fully understands the dynamics of depression. If you believe that your symptoms match any described in this chapter, consult a medical professional immediately.

Signs of Depression

⇝ Depressed or irritable mood most of the time

⇝ A diminished interest in normal activities

⇝ Decrease or increase in appetite

⇝ Insomnia or hypersomnia

⇝ Fatigue

- Showing no interest in pleasurable activity

- Restlessness or agitation

- Overwhelming feelings of worthlessness or guilt

- Lack of concentration

- Indecisiveness

- Thoughts of death and suicide

- Loss of energy

Suicide

Suicide is an all-too-real aspect of bipolar disorder. According to Dr. Kay Redfield Jamison in *Night Falls Fast: Understanding Suicide,* many people ignore the biological causes of suicide. She explains, "Ninety to 95 percent of suicides are caused by illness—common illnesses that can be helped by medication. Depression is common, drug abuse is common, manic-depression is real common. But the public doesn't tie them to suicide."

The suicide rate among young people has tripled during the past forty years; it is now the second leading cause of death among college students. Only one in four leaves behind a clearly written explanation of their intentions. Most people are still afraid to openly discuss suicide, and, as a consequence, suicide remains hidden from public view. As Jamison explains, "It is a societal illusion that suicide is rare. It is not. Every seventeen minutes in America someone commits suicide."

Throughout their lives, many people commonly consider suicide, and not all of them suffer from bipolar disorder. Teenagers are especially plagued with suicidal thoughts and these should be taken very seriously. For every adolescent suicide completed, there may be twenty or more attempts, and reports estimate that 50 percent of students in an average American classroom have considered taking their own lives.

Often times, individuals living with bipolar disorder find themselves falling into a sinkhole of despair. They become exasperated from dealing with the constant discord in their lives. Consequently, suicidal thoughts among manic-depressives can become urgent and tireless. Further, for the bipolar individual, suicide becomes a choice that he or she believes will save others from suffering. It is just this type of obsessive thinking that leads a person to contemplate ending his or her life.

Warning Signs

Suicide can be prevented in most cases. In others, however, people are powerless to stop suicidal behaviors. The key to suicide prevention is listening to and interpreting its warning signs, however subtle. Changes in behavior such as reckless driving, increased risk-taking, social withdrawal, giving away valued possessions, heavy drinking or drug use, or the casual handling of weapons can all be warning signs. If you think someone you know might be suicidal, stay mindful of discussions or the mere mention of death or suicide. Listen for innuendoes that refer to his or her future absence, such as "You'll remember me when you celebrate the holidays," or "Light a candle for me on my birthday." Of course, any open threats of suicide should be taken very seriously. If you have any reason to believe that a person is considering suicide as a way out of hopeless or helpless feelings, help him or her find professional help immediately. Other immediate actions you might consider include:

⇝ Removing anything that could be used as an obvious weapon: knives, razors, guns, rope, even vehicles

⇝ Searching for any stash of drugs or alcohol that could be taken as an overdose

⇝ Calmly communicating your concern for the individual; maintaining a nonjudgmental attitude

⇝ Considering the option of constant supervision

Suicide can and should be prevented. Current medical reports indicate that most, if not all, suicides have a biological link to certain mental illnesses such as bipolar or unipolar depression. Medical professionals can remedy these illnesses before desperate individuals commit suicide. Similar to how both electroconvulsive therapy and the drug lithium have a dramatically positive effect on bipolar disorder, both treatments can help patients who obsessively contemplate suicide.

Bipolar Disorder

Within the general category of bipolar disorder, there are several subcategories, or types, of bipolar disorders. These types include bipolar I, bipolar II, cyclothymic, and rapid-cycling bipolar disorder. Doctors use these distinctions to more accurately diagnose patients according to the range and severity of symptoms they present.

Bipolar I

Think of bipolar I as classic manic-depression: full-blown manic attacks followed by, though sometimes not immediately, deep depressions. Bipolar disorder is among the most unique of all mental disorders simply because it relapses, or goes into long periods of regression on its own without warning. This may happen with or without treatment. Physicians consider this its tendency to "hibernate."

In 1942, the *American Journal of Psychiatry* published a study on the unpredictability of bipolar disorder: Sixty-six patients, all suffering from manic-depression, were studied for a period of twenty-six years. Some patients reported having had only one episode of depression or mania, while one-third reported having four to six episodes, and another third had at least seven episodes. According to the same study, the average duration of each episode was about six months. Medical professionals now know that the average duration of a manic or depressive episode as experienced by a person suffering with bipolar disorder without treatment is six to eight months. However, manic and depressive states may be much shorter or much longer in length depending on the individual and the severity of his or her illness.

Bipolar II

Deep, dark depressions and episodes of hypomania most often characterize bipolar II. Bipolar II is a calmer or softer version of bipolar I. Bipolar II patients almost never have full-blown manic episodes and they do not tend to feel completely out of control. Currently, statistics show that fewer than 5 percent of all bipolar patients fall into this category.

Bipolar II became a viable diagnosis in the 1970s, when psychiatrists started to prescribe lithium as an all-purpose drug for the disorder. Researchers and doctors alike now believe that bipolar II is not a precursor to bipolar I, but its own distinct, simpler, and milder mental illness. Some also contend that bipolar II is more widespread. Its symptoms, similar to its more severe counterpart, have been described as follows: full-blown depressive episodes followed by shorter episodes of hypomania, increased need for sleep during episodes of depression, and a family history of depression. Bipolar II individuals have also shown an increased incidence of alcoholism.

Conclusive studies also indicate that individuals experiencing bipolar II often have an immediate family member who suffers from deep depression and mild mania. There are, however, a few generalized symptoms of bipolar II. Many patients, most of whom never fully comprehend their subtle mood swings, firmly believe that they suffer from clinical or unipolar depression. Bipolar II individuals tend to spend the majority of their lives coping with dark episodes of depression. These periods are only sometimes interrupted by comparatively shorter moments of euphoria and activity.

Many scientists now believe that individuals afflicted with bipolar II may have only one gene linked to mood disorders, whereas individuals with bipolar I (a much more complex mental disorder) may have inherited multiple genes linked to mood disorders. Currently, researchers believe that not every person who is genetically susceptible to bipolar disorder will develop the illness. Again, it is also important to remember that environmental influences affect the development and onset of any mental disorder. For instance, although an individual may be generally predisposed to bipolar illness, he or she may not develop the disease in the same manner as another individual with a similar genetic composition. People experience bipolar disorder as individuals partly because of their environments and the stress-inducing situations that they encounter. This factor is often overlooked by patients. Bipolar disorder is often influenced by stress, anxiety, and other environmental factors, some of which may be controlled. Studies also indicate that environmental factors may include prolonged exposure to strong light sources, sleep reduction, childbirth, or drug and alcohol abuse.

Cyclothymic Disorder

As bipolar II is considered a milder version of bipolar I, cyclothymic disorder exhibits many of the symptoms of bipolar II, but in a much milder form and during a more rapid cycle. For years, doctors classified cyclothymic disorder as a personality rather than a mood disorder because its mild mood swings, although rapid indeed, were separated by short periods (usually less than two months) of relative normalcy.

Cyclothymic disorder is punctuated by very short episodes of hypomania that are then followed by very brief periods of depression. To be diagnosed as suffering from cyclothymic disorder, patients need to exhibit these dramatic fluctuations for at least two years. Children and adolescents can be classified as cyclothymic after only one year, however. Mood cycles, swinging back and forth between manic and depressive episodes, can last for a few days or up to several weeks and are not considered severe or fully developed. These cyclical periods of depression and mania are regular and begin during adolescence or in the early twenties. Sometimes these mood swings from high to low can be extremely rapid— changing from a mild euphoric state to a depressed mood in a twenty-four-hour period. It is often normal for the cyclothymic individual to retire to sleep feeling low and then awaken abuzz with activity.

Normally, people who are constantly under the influence of a rapidly changeable mood have an unstable sense of self. They constantly fluctuate from states of little self-confidence to being overly confident. One day a cyclothymic individual might seem aggressive and the next withdrawn; the quality of work in his or her professional life may be uneven. In fact, this inconsistency is pervasive: He or she will have repeated shifts of attitude toward nearly every aspect of his or her life, work, study, interests, or future plans. Approximately 6 percent of individuals suffering from cyclothymic disorder will see their illness develop into bipolar I or bipolar II, especially if they are carelessly and inconsistently taking medications for the illness.

Rapid-Cycling Disorder

Doctors coined the term "rapid-cycling disorder" to identify bipolar patients who experienced four or more episodes of depression or mania in a one-year period. As some thyroid conditions have been proven to exhibit similar symptoms, doctors need to rule out the presence of other medical conditions that might also cause frequent emotional swings. Interestingly, most patients exhibiting signs of rapid-cycling disorder are female—nearly three-quarters in most studies. This is in marked contrast to the breakdown among bipolar I and II patients: 50 percent male, 50 percent female. Also, rapid-cycling patients almost always have relatives who are afflicted with mood disorders. Rapid-cycling usually begins with a depressive episode rather than a manic one, and is far less responsive to lithium—a mood-stabilizing drug commonly prescribed to patients coping with bipolar disorder. Physicians have recognized rapid-cycling disorder as a lithium-resistant subgroup since the 1970s. Therefore it is much more difficult to treat. Although some rapid-cycling patients do respond to lithium and other mood-stabilizing drugs, rapid-cycling bipolar individuals are still considered among those most treatment-resistant.

Many doctors now believe that rapid-cycling bipolar disorder is not its own disease, but a specific phase within the life and progression of bipolar disorder. Medical professionals have yet to identify why some patients with bipolar I or II disorder develop rapid-cycling symptoms, but they suspect that antidepressant medications might play a role. Physicians worldwide have repeatedly found that antidepressants increase manic episodes for patients stricken with rapid-cycling disorder. That is why it is important to speak frankly with medical professionals regarding bipolar symptoms. Even slight suggestions of unusual behavior may alert mental-health professionals to a clearer understanding of a person's state of mind. As with any mental disorder, a clear diagnosis is the first step toward recovery. This is especially true concerning the subtle distinctions of bipolar disorder.

Bipolar Spectrum Disorders or Shadow Syndromes

Psychiatrists use the term "bipolar spectrum disorder" to describe a patient who has a marked tendency toward bipolar symptoms, but whose condition is not indicative of bipolar I, bipolar II, or cyclothymia. For years, clinicians have recognized these moderate forms of bipolar, usually referring to them as pseudo-unipolar depression, or bipolar III. The striking pattern among patients diagnosed with bipolar spectrum disorders is a history of depressive-like or manic-like tendencies within their normal mood state. What finally makes these individuals' symptoms prominent is a heightened level of mood—

whether manic or depressive. Usually, this intense state of either depression or mania forces the bipolar spectrum patient to seek treatment.

In general, individuals with bipolar spectrum disorders or bipolar III have a temperament that is "higher" than most people, that is to say, they are full of energy, cheerful, talkative, very sociable, and confident. Psychiatrists call this a hyperthymic temperament. The hyperthymic personality is also impulsive and disappoints easily—often to the point of irritability, anger, or recklessness. Common traits attributed to bipolar III individuals are an extroverted personality, a tendency to suffer recurrent depressions, a family history of depression, and requiring less than six hours of sleep per twenty-four-hour period.

Seasonal Affective Disorder

Seasonal affective disorder, or SAD, is now thought to affect some 9 to 15 percent of individuals who are coping with some form of depressive illness, including bipolar disorder. These individuals tend to live closer to the poles of Earth, where variations in daylight are extreme. Scientists do not classify SAD as a separate disorder. They do, however, consider SAD an aspect of bipolar disorder and depression, generally. Again, some research points to the availability of light levels to be a chief environmental factor of the disorder.

SAD also refers to a seasonal pattern in any mental illness. For instance, a person may be classified as bipolar I, with a seasonal pattern. The seasonal pattern portion of this diagnosis refers to SAD—a depression that has several obvious symptoms, such as low energy levels, hypersomnia, cravings for carbohydrates such as pasta, sweets, and bread, weight gain, and typical afternoon or evening sluggishness.

Now, although that list of symptoms sounds very much like the symptoms associated with depression and the depressive episodes of bipolar disorder, individuals diagnosed with SAD respond favorably to a very specific treatment called light therapy, or photo therapy. During photo therapy treatment, patients are exposed to bright light boxes during the morning or evening hours. Depending on the severity of his or her symptoms, it could take up to several weeks before a patient responds to photo therapy.

Commonly, individuals with SAD suffer from severe winter depressions and summer manias or mood elevations. Unfortunately, scientists do not yet understand why certain individuals react to seasonal changes in natural light. Some believe that SAD is caused by malfunctions in the body's internal biological clock, or that these patients are abnormally sensitive to light. What scientists do know is that serotonin—a neurotransmitter that affects depression— works seasonally and is at its lowest levels in the body during the months of December and January of each year.

Bipolar Disorder and the Brain

Many physical changes occur in the body of a person who suffers from depression or mood disorders such as bipolar. Researchers associate these changes with neurons, or tiny nerve cells, inside the human brain. Each of the estimated 11 million neurons in the brain functions like a computer processor, receiving input from other neurons. Each neuron can process and program messages to thousands of other neurons, potentially helping to send and receive information. This information tells the body how to feel, to think, and to function.

Scientists now believe that the function of some neurons within the brains of individuals suffering from bipolar disorder is defective. Additionally, people may suffer from bipolar disorder due to malfunctions in the brain's chemical signaling system. The human brain uses molecular chemical signals, called neurotransmitters, that promote communication between neurons. The neurons send these chemical signals across synapses. The microscopic space between the two neurons at the synapse site is called the synaptic cleft. Think of one neuron, the one sending the chemical and electrical message to the other, as the presynaptic neuron. These messages flow from the presynaptic neuron across the synaptic cleft, to the next neuron, the receptor, or postsynaptic neuron.

Just as a computer is programmed and reprogrammed with information, each neuron must be cleaned out or cleared of old information to make room for the next set of instructions. This is a constant process. One way the brain does this is through what is known as the reuptake method. There is a reuptake pump located on the presynaptic neuron (the neuron that sends the message). This pump removes neurotransmitters from the synapse and reprograms them so that they are released from the synapse. To put it simply, in bipolar patients there is a decreased level of neurotransmitters in the synapse.

However, this is not the only, nor is it a complete explanation of what causes bipolar disorder. Scientists have also discovered that brain malfunctions within bipolar patients may have many different chemical sources. The combination of these chemicals may produce manic and depressive episodes.

Bipolar Genetics

For nearly a century, both physicians and scientists have suspected that a dramatic link between mental illness and heredity exists. In 1904, Emil Kraeplin noted in several studies that manic-depressive illnesses affected some families over the course of several generations. However, for a very long time, this type of generalized information was all that the world of science could offer in terms of a genetic explanation of mental illness.

Genes provide the blueprint for mental and physical development. Genes are special codes that determine a person's traits and bodily development. Researchers have been able to isolate and identify a number of genes that may be linked to bipolar disorder. In the coming years, it is hoped that scientists will be able to isolate all the genes that are likely to store information about this mental illness, but these studies are in the early stages.

Significantly, bipolar disorder occurs in only a fraction of the individuals at genetic risk. If both parents are bipolar, the risk of developing the disease is greater than if only one parent has the disease. The more individuals within a family that have mental illnesses, such as unipolar depression, schizophrenia, or other mood disorders, the greater the chances are that a child born into that family will develop some form of mental illness.

However, some would argue that this correlation is attributable to the strong environmental influence of the family and is not due only to genetic predisposition.

Testing for Bipolar Disorder?

Presently, a diagnostic test for bipolar disorder does not exist. According to Fred Petty, professor of psychiatry at the University of Texas Southwestern Medical School, such tests are being developed. "My laboratory has published some work looking at the blood levels of an amino acid called GABA (gamma amino butyric acid), which functions as a neurotransmitter in the brain. Bipolar patients often show low levels of GABA in the bloodstream," he explains. Although this test is only being used in research, it could lead to the creation of a generalized test for bipolar disorder, or perhaps a method of detecting the presence of bipolar genes in the body.

Seeking Professional Help

It can be quite difficult to diagnose and treat precisely any mental illness. Instead, doctors frequently evaluate a person's mental state by asking many questions and scrutinizing the physical and psychological status of the patient over time. Doctors might also rely on psychological tests, mental status examinations, and family history.

The road to an accurate diagnosis is rarely short or direct. By definition, bipolar disorder is highly individualistic. A person's symptoms might seem obvious or surface only occasionally. Because of the difficulty involved in diagnosis, many people suffering from bipolar disorder are misdiagnosed with schizophrenia, unipolar depression, or a personality disorder. If you or someone you know thinks he or she might have bipolar disorder, find a medical professional that you trust and openly discuss your feelings with him or her. Establishing this relationship will pave the way to effective treatment.

The Good News

Treatment is available to everyone who suffers from bipolar disorder. This treatment often involves medications. The need for bipolar patients to take daily medications such as mood-stabilizing drugs should not be underestimated. Mood stabilizers such as lithium are still the most effective and most

widely used treatment for this disease. Along with drug therapy, psychotherapy also plays an important role in treatment.
With treatment, success rates for controlling the mood
swings associated with bipolar disorder are as high as 80 percent. Probably the greatest challenge faced by those who
may be bipolar, however, is recognizing the need for treatment and maintaining that treatment over the course of their
entire lives. Many individuals simply discontinue drug treatments when their moods return to normal. This is a very dangerous choice. Others discontinue medications in order to
recapture a higher mood, or what bipolar patients sometimes
refer to as their more "spirited" moods. For these patients,
soft or milder forms of mania hardly seem like an affliction.
Periods of soft mania enable some bipolar individuals to
work excessive hours, maintain a higher level of productivity,
and reach seemingly compelling and insightful conclusions
about life. However, the down side of bipolar disorder—its
lower, darker, depressive episodes—send many clutching for
answers, and, finally, treatment.

As a teenager, it is very difficult to recognize whether
one's moodiness is more extreme than the hormonally
induced mood swings of adolescence. Therefore,
although symptoms of bipolar disorder may be exhibited
during adolescence, unless they are very dramatic, they
often go unnoticed.

Often, teenagers will act out and adults may mis-
interpret their behavior. Teens may miss school, disrupt
normal activities, or become increasingly antisocial.
Any sudden changes in behavior should be examined
and considered.

It is difficult for doctors to diagnose bipolar disorder in
both teens and adults simply because its symptoms can

mirror chronic depression or even, at times, schizophrenia, if the individual is diagnosed during an acute manic episode. During an initial consultation, a doctor might attempt to zero in on the causes of a person's mental health problem. If the patient is depressed, could he or she be suffering from unipolar depression? Is there a history of depression in this person's family? How long has the person felt this way? How is he or she describing his or her depressive feelings and emotions? Does the individual experience mood swings, and if so, to what extent? Other behavioral signs should also be examined: school or job performance, socialization skills, and the ability to maintain relationships, both within the family unit and outside the home.

As you can see, diagnosing bipolar disorder is anything but simple. Doctors must form a relationship with the patient and must understand his or her habits before reaching a conclusion. A doctor gains the most insight into a patient's condition when a patient is open and honest about his or her feelings and explains them in the greatest detail possible. This renders a more complete picture of a patient's mental health. However, a doctor will prescribe medication immediately if he or she feels that the patient is in danger.

Professional Help

When you consider seeking counseling for a mood disorder, you can consult your family doctor. He or she may be familiar with your medical history, or may have a colleague in the mental health profession. Some doctors may recommend talk therapy, such as psychotherapy; the majority will prescribe medication for bipolar disorder.

Family Physicians

Your family physician can prescribe medication for bipolar disorder, but bear in mind that he or she is not trained to treat complex mood disorders. Treatment with a psychologist or psychiatrist is much more effective. After an initial consultation with your family doctor, you may need to see someone who is specially trained in mood disorders and who can determine which type of drug treatment would be most beneficial. Typically, physicians review a patient's family history and then refer him or her to a specialist.

Psychologists and Psychiatrists

Psychologists and psychiatrists are trained therapists who help people cope with and solve their problems. The main difference between the two is that a psychiatrist is also a physician with a medical degree. Consequently, he or she can prescribe medications, such as antidepressants. Before you decide whether to see a psychologist or psychiatrist, you should evaluate how you feel about chemical treatments. Spend time with your doctor and ask him or her to explain why drug therapy is necessary. Chances are, he or she will outline a variety of available drug treatments and their side effects. In nearly every case, doctors treat individuals afflicted with bipolar disorder with a combination of drugs that includes a mood stabilizer, an antidepressant, and occasionally, an antipsychotic, as needed. Drug treatments will be thoroughly discussed in the following chapters.

Professional Degrees

As you investigate therapists, you will discover a wide array of initials after their names; these signify academic degrees, licenses, and certifications earned. When searching for a therapist, look for someone with a master's degree or a doctorate in a mental health field. This demonstrates that he or she has had advanced and specific training about psychological problems and that he or she will understand the subtleties of mood disorders. Some of these professional degrees are:

M.D. (Psychiatrist—Doctor of Medicine): This means that the doctor has received his or her medical degree and has had four years of clinical residency practicing as a psychiatrist. M.D.'s can prescribe medication.

Ph.D. (Doctor of Philosophy) and Psy.D. (Doctor of Psychology): These professionals have had four to six years of graduate study. They frequently work in schools, businesses, mental health centers, and hospitals.

M.A. (Master of Arts degree in psychology): This is basically a counseling degree. Therapists with this degree have a background in psychotherapy and clinical experience.

M.S. (Master of Science degree in psychology): Professionals with this degree typically focus on research in a specific subject area.

Ed.D. (Doctor of Education): This degree indicates that an individual has a background in education, child development, and general psychology.

M.S.W. (Master of Social Work): This is a social-work degree that prepares an individual to diagnose and treat psychological problems and provide mental-health referrals. Psychiatric social workers constitute the single largest group of mental health professionals.

Remember that just because a medical or counseling professional has impressive degrees, it does not mean that he or she is necessarily the right therapist for you. It is crucial that you feel comfortable with your therapist so that you can talk openly and honestly about your experiences. Ideally, you will feel comfortable detailing how you may have felt while suffering from manic or depressive episodes. If you are uncomfortable speaking about the intimate details of your life with a therapist, your treatment will not be as effective.

Types of Therapy

There are many approaches to talk therapy, including group therapy, psychoanalysis, family therapy, and individual therapy. Some approaches may be helpful to you. Others may not. Developing an honest relationship with your therapist and believing in his or her ability to guide you through recovery is very important. Two of the most common individual therapies include cognitive therapy and cognitive-behavioral therapy. Seeing a psychiatrist is strongly recommended for treating bipolar disorder, however.

Cognitive Therapy

Cognitive therapy is a form of therapy that is commonly used to treat people suffering with depression, not mood disorders such as bipolar disorder. However, some mental health professionals agree that recognizing the negative thought patterns that characterize the depressive state of bipolar disorder is a worthwhile addition to drug treatment. Cognitive therapy is firmly based in the idea that you are what you think. If a person repeatedly thinks that he or she is not good enough, he or she will suffer from low self-esteem. In cognitive therapy, people articulate their negative thought patterns and then identify the causes of those thought patterns.

Cognitive-Behavioral Therapy

Cognitive-behavioral therapy relies on the techniques of cognitive therapy, and it also focuses on decreasing or changing specific behaviors that spark or further exaggerate manic or depressive episodes. These behaviors might include poor sleeping and eating habits or the recreational use of drugs or alcohol. The goal of cognitive-behavioral therapy is to teach patients to recognize triggers that set mood swings in motion and ultimately, to prevent full-blown episodes of depression or mania.

The Advent of Modern Drug Therapies: Mood Stabilizers

Bipolar patients must make an important choice every day of their lives: choose to remain on the mood-stabilizing medications that help them control their emotions, or ignore their need for drug therapy and suffer an eventual, or sometimes immediate, relapse. Doctors cannot predict how severe mood disorders will become, nor can they fully explain why bipolar disorder recedes. Drug remedies are not always easy and quick. Sometimes, doctors must prescribe several drugs, or drug combinations, before the most effective regime is found. When it is, though, it can be lifesaving. Although many different medications relieve the symptoms of bipolar disorder, they fall into three main categories: mood stabilizers, antidepressants, and antipsychotics. All of these drugs affect the chemicals in the brain called neurotransmitters.

Jamie

My treatment is like a resisted reality. I never want it, yet I know that I truly need it. After a particularly bad phase of depression or mania, medications stabilize me, and my life improves. Then, as soon as my symptoms are gone, I believe there is no need for the medications anymore. I am bipolar-free. This thought is the greatest illusion. Bipolar disorder is not curable.

55

It is treatable. The illusion is that the best strategy is to discontinue taking medications. Actually, the drugs make me feel healthy. Sometimes my thinking becomes too clouded to see that. Unfortunately, being free of this illness is also an illusion.

Mood Stabilizers

In most cases, if a psychiatrist believes that a person is suffering from bipolar disorder, he or she will prescribe a mood-stabilizing medication. The number of new mood-stabilizing medications has increased dramatically in recent years. Twenty years ago, lithium was the only drug available that helped to level the highs and lows of bipolar disorder.

Mood stabilizers have the ability to decrease not only the severity of manic and depressive episodes, but also their frequency. In addition to drug remedies, electro-convulsive therapy (ECT) is also considered a mood stabilizer. ECT will be discussed in a later chapter.

Initially, the effects of some mood stabilizers may not be evident for several weeks. If a patient is experiencing an acute episode of mania, doctors often prescribe other drugs to help decrease insomnia, (sedatives such as benzodiazepine) or antipsychotics (Zyprexa, Seroquel, Risperdal, and clozapine). Doctors refer to these drugs as adjunctive medications because they are a part of an overall drug regimen. In fact, drug combinations are a common treatment for bipolar disorder.

Lithium

For years, lithium has been known to assist people who struggle with mood swings. Doctors are now certain that lithium is a more appropriate medication than are other mood stabilizers for individuals who are experiencing pure mania, or mania without depression. Lithium is far less effective for people experiencing mixed-manic states or rapid-cycling bipolar disorder, however.

Taking lithium may cause side effects such as an increased need to urinate, thirst, and water retention. Usually, reducing the dosage can eliminate these problems. To do this, doctors gradually decrease the dosage amounts until the least amount of an effective dose is established. Other side effects can include nausea, diarrhea, hand tremors, and weight gain. In fact, because of side effects and other problems associated with lithium, its use must be carefully monitored. The difference between the medicinal level and the toxic level of lithium is so small that doctors and patients take great care when using the drug. Doctors conduct routine blood tests to verify levels of lithium in the body. Like many mood stabilizers, lithium has been associated with birth defects. Doctors advise women to practice birth control while taking such drugs. Women who suspect they are pregnant and who are currently taking lithium should contact their doctor immediately.

Between 5 and 35 percent of lithium users also develop hypothyroidism. Hypothyroidism occurs when the thyroid gland malfunctions and thyroid function becomes depressed. When carefully monitored by doctors, though, this too can be treated. Other patients complain of a decrease in mental function, or a "dulling" of the senses, kidney malfunction, and persistent skin problems. For these reasons, doctors try to prescribe the lowest possible dosage of any drug.

Lithium: The Bipolar Wonder Drug

Raise the subject of the medication lithium (also known by the brand names Eskalith, Lithobid, and Lithonate) and you may raise an eyebrow. Most bipolar patients have been successfully treated using this drug, although it is a vintage remedy compared with the many new mood-stabilizing medications that are currently available. Even now, more than thirty years since its debut as a treatment, lithium is still recommended for a majority of people coping with bipolar disorder. Some patients complain of vicious side effects, however, and, as a result, they stay on, and then go off, the medication. This erratic intake sends these patients spiraling back into escalating mood cycles.

Is lithium a bipolar patient's wonder pill? Actually, it is nothing more than an alkali metal and the lightest of the solid elements. Discovered in 1817 by a Swedish chemistry student, lithium was first used in the treatment of gout, but later was touted as a wonder cure-all. Natural waters found to contain high concentrations of the metal were even bottled as Bear Lithia Water and were sold as an elixir until many reported feeling no reaction to the concoction. Still, European and American mineral waters containing lithium were advertised as a natural treatment which promoted one's physical and mental health.

Over a century later, in 1949, lithium was found to contain properties that combat the effects of mania. John E. Cade, an Australian psychiatrist, made this accidental discovery when he used lithium salt to suspend uric acid. He realized that lithium had antimania properties when he injected the mixture into guinea pigs and found that they reacted by feeling calm. He then administered the drug to manic patients and had dramatically successful results. As lithium gained respect in other parts of the world, physicians and patients in the United States remained skeptical. This skepticism seemed well-founded when later in 1949, high doses of lithium caused the deaths of several cardiac patients. One medical report found that high doses of lithium were toxic. In 1970, lithium finally received approval in the United States from the Food and Drug Administration (FDA) as a mood disorder treatment. Still, consumers remained somewhat reluctant to trust the natural drug. Unfortunately, many, if not most, bipolar patients simply discontinue medication at will—an extremely dangerous act. According to a 1999 report in the *Journal of the American Medical Association*, "Interruption of (lithium) treatment is a common occurrence in patients with bipolar disorder, and some reports suggest that discontinuation and resumption of lithium also can lessen the drug's efficacy." Lithium is still an effective preventative medication for those suffering with classic bipolar symptoms, especially individuals who might be at a higher risk for suicide. Studies have demonstrated conclusively lithium's anti-aggressive properties. It has also been proven to help curb suicidal thoughts in bipolar patients.

Charles

Because I'm a teenager, my parents thought my depression was a normal rite of passage. If I became manic, they assumed that I was making up for all the months I had stayed in bed. It was only after I started taking lithium that my moods finally calmed. I'm finally in control.

Valproate

Valproate, sold under the brand names Divalproex, Depakote, or Depakene, was first used to treat individuals suffering from epileptic seizures in the 1960s. Although the exact therapeutic effects of valproate are still unknown, the drug seems to improve the transmission of information between neurons. More specifically, it improves neuronal transmission of the chemical neurotransmitter gamma amino butyric acid (GABA), a chemical that seems to balance different brain circuits. Like lithium, valproate decreases the severity and frequency of manic episodes, but it is far less effective in treating depression.

The body responds quickly to valproate, especially as compared to lithium. Valproate helps modulate the mood swings of those suffering with rapid-cycling bipolar disorder. It also helps eliminate mixed-manic symptoms and is far less toxic than lithium.

Still, doctors must also monitor levels of valproate in the blood. Patients taking valproate should be aware of potential liver problems and should watch for signs of liver damage, such as unusual bleeding or bruising and jaundice (yellowing of the eyes and skin), fever, and water retention. Because the drug is less useful in the treatment of depressive episodes, physicians prescribe it to treat the milder bipolar disorders: cyclothymia and bipolar II. Valproate is less toxic than lithium, and its side effects are also less extreme but may include stomach upset, sleepiness, weight gain, increased appetite, hand tremors, and in some patients, hair loss.

Carbamazepine

Commonly known by the brand names Tegretol, Carbatrol, and Epitol, carbamazepine, like valproate, was introduced to the public in the 1960s as a drug that could control seizures in epileptic patients. Shortly thereafter, however, researchers in Japan noted the drug's use in treating individuals with bipolar symptoms. Some treatment-resistant patients have shown a marked improvement when carbamazepine is administered. For other patients, carbamazepine is a "second-line" mood stabilizer, used in combination with lithium, valproate, or antipsychotic medications.

There are few side effects associated with carbamazepine. They are sleepiness, lightheadedness, and some initial nausea. Adjusting the dosage modifies most reactions. Carbamazepine does have one very severe, potential side effect: A very small percentage of individuals taking carbamazepine have developed a dangerous skin reaction to it called Stevens-Johnson syndrome. As a result, all patients taking this drug should be on the lookout for the development of rashes, a yellowing of the skin, bleeding, bruising, water retention, or signs of infection.

Lamotrigine

Doctors are excited about lamotrigine because it has both antimanic and antidepressant effects. Other studies have indicated that lamotrigine, when taken in combination with other mood stabilizers, has helped formerly treatment-resistant patients. Lamotrigine is non-toxic so monitoring its level in the bloodstream is unncessary. Lamotrigine decreases the release of a certain neurotransmitter called glutamate. Glutamate is an amino acid that reportedly causes the stimulation of several neural circuits. Lamotrigine also reportedly affects at least one of the brain's messenger systems (like lithium), called the inositol triphosphate system. In general, it has fewer side effects than do other mood-stabilizing medications. Overall, side effects include headaches, sleepiness, and nausea. Significantly, unlike many of its sister medications, lamotrigine has no longstanding effect on the liver or kidneys. However, as with carbamazepine, patients should watch for changes in skin tone and condition. Doctors instruct patients to stop taking lamotrigine immediately if any changes in skin condition occur. Lamotrigine is prescribed only for patients over the age of sixteen.

Gabapentin

Gabapentin, also known as Neurontin, is a relatively new mood stabilizer and one for which little research has been completed. It appears useful in combating symptoms of anxiety and it rarely interacts negatively with other medications. The side effects from gabapentin can include fatigue, sedation, and dizziness.

Topiramate

Research on this anticonvulsant mood stabilizer, also known as Topamax, has revealed that it reduces the effects of acute manic symptoms. Unlike many other mood-stabilizing medications, topiramate does not appear to cause significant weight gain. Its side effects can include sedation, dizziness, memory loss, and a dulling of the senses.

Christopher

I am currently under the care of a skilled psychiatrist. He treats my bipolar symptoms with Tegretol and Wellbutrin. He had to add Trazadone at night to ease my anxiety but finally I am stable. Most people do not know that I suffer from this disease. Now, with medication, I can live a normal life.

Antidepressants, Antipsychotics, and Other Treatments

Antidepressants

Researchers classify antidepressants according to their chemical properties. Generally, there are three types of antidepressants: tricyclics, selective serotonin reuptake inhibitors (SSRIs), and monoamine oxidase inhibitors (MAOIs). In addition to prescribing a mood-stabilizing drug like lithium, carbamazepine, or lamotrigine, a doctor will most likely prescribe an antidepressant to help alleviate symptoms of bipolar-related depression. Both doctor and patient should remain aware of the increased risk of slipping into a manic state while taking these drugs, however. According to a number of major studies, antidepressants, in the process of lifting a person out of a depressive state, can propel a patient into a manic episode if he or she already has an underlying bipolar illness.

Consequently, doctors almost always prescribe antidepressants in combination with mood-stabilizing medications. Antidepressants often take several weeks before they begin altering brain chemistry. It is also common for patients to try several types of antidepressants before finding the most effective medication. Drug therapy can be very successful, but finding the correct medication or combination of medications can become a tedious and tiresome affair for patients. Many people who are coping with bipolar disorder become discouraged. It is for this reason that individuals should understand completely the importance of remaining on medications and following any medical instructions.

Sheila

Being diagnosed with bipolar disorder can be extremely traumatic. I have been on and off medications for manic-depression several times. You can reach a point in your recovery when you believe you are stable. After getting stabilized on medications and having my normal moods return, I was able to put my life back together. Then I believed that I would be fine without medication. I quit taking it. I have done this several times—at seventeen, nineteen, twenty, and twenty-three years of age. Now I know never to do it again. In many instances, mania and depression do not return immediately after you stop taking your medications, but they do return. Although it feels like the most difficult thing you have ever done, you have to pick up the telephone, call a psychiatrist, and admit that you need chemical help. I realized that I have a flaw in my brain that I cannot willfully change.

Generally, antidepressants enable more of the necessary chemicals—serotonin, dopamine, and norepinephrine—to pool around nerve synapses in the brain. In this way, less of the neurotransmitter is reabsorbed. For instance, antidepressants like Prozac increase the level of serotonin in the brain. It is theorized that depressed individuals have less of these chemicals that help steady thoughts and emotions.

Unfortunately, antidepressants are less than effective for approximately 30 percent of patients. Because of this, your doctor may experiment with different drugs in varying combinations until he or she finds the best treatment. Patients can find this experience exhausting and aggravating, but it is important to remain hopeful and to keep an open mind about drug therapy. More often than not, antidepressants save lives and should be considered an effective treatment option when combined with a mood stabilizer by those suffering from a mood disorder such as bipolar.

Tricyclics

Among the first antidepressants developed, tricyclics have a three-part (tri-) chemical structure. Tricyclic antidepressants inhibit the reuptake of the chemical or neurotransmitter norepinephrine. In some instances, tricyclics affect the chemical levels of serotonin. When a tricyclic antidepressant does its job correctly, the chemical norepinephrine remains in the neuron a bit longer, prolonging its work (or the message that it is sending) in the cell. Of course, the work that is done by the intake of tricyclics into the brain is a very complex process; this brief explanation is to allow for a general understanding of the action of the medication on brain activity.

Because the side effects of tricyclic medications can be irritating to some patients, they are prescribed less often than other antidepressants. However, tricyclic drugs do work well for some individuals, especially when other antidepressants have failed. Because tricyclics also block another neurotransmitter, acetylcholine, (integral to the body's digestive functions) taking them could cause a slowing of the digestive process resulting in constipation.

Other potential side effects can include dry mouth, dizziness, temporary loss of focus, weight gain, and painful urination. Tricyclic medications must be carefully monitored, because increased dosages can sometimes become toxic.

Selective Serotonin Reuptake Inhibitors

First making an appearance in 1988, selective serotonin reuptake inhibitors (SSRIs), especially Prozac, caused a sensation when approved by the Food and Drug Administration (FDA). Medications in the SSRI family include not only Prozac (fluoxetine), but also Luvox (fluvoxamine), Paxil (paroxetine), Zoloft (sertraline), and Effexor (venlafaxine). Because SSRIs caused virtually none of the side effects that tricyclics did, they were widely accepted by the public. Unlike tricyclics, which affect levels of the neurotransmitter norepinephrine, SSRIs block the release of another neurotransmitter, serotonin. The chemical action of this drug is very specific, blocking the reuptake of serotonin without altering any other brain chemistry.

The main side effects of SSRIs are stomach upset and sexual dysfunction. Additionally, patients have complained that they feel overstimulated when taking SSRIs. As a result, SSRIs can curb hunger, can increase the need for exercise, and can cause weight loss. Peter D. Kramer, in his best-selling book, *Listening to Prozac*, explains a potentially severe side effect of SSRIs, specifically Prozac: "Mania is an infrequent (but) bad outcome of taking Prozac. Although there is scant data on the subject, many psychiatrists believe Prozac causes this side effect more frequently than tricyclic antidepressants."

Prozac, the Patented Mood Pill

Probably the most famous, well-known antidepressant is the tiny, blue pill created in the mid-1980s. Just two years after it hit the U.S. market in 1989, more than 65,000 prescriptions were being filled monthly for this celebrated drug. Prozac reportedly left patients feeling much better than usual.

In contrast, some people took exception to the way the production of Prozac became monopolized by one company, Eli Lilly. The Drug Price Competition and Patent Term Act of 1984 not only made it easier for consumers to buy generic drugs, but also extended patent protection to Eli Lilly to produce Prozac an extra five years, guaranteeing the company a monopoly on the market that resulted in enormous profits.

Subsequently, reports of complications with Prozac arose in the media. Doctors reported that some patients found the drug depersonalizing and that they suffered from an increased sense of alienation. Many of these same patients also sought to end their own lives. Some independent studies now report that Prozac does cause an increase in suicidal thoughts in a small percentage of patients (approximately 7 percent) with strong antisocial thought patterns. In fact, Eli Lilly was sued in the mid-1990s for not warning the public of Prozac's potential side effects. Some of these suits claimed that mentally ill patients exhibited strong violent behavior just weeks after taking the drug. Now, both doctors and patients are aware of the potential benefits and risks of Prozac.

Monoamine Oxidase Inhibitors

Researchers discovered Parnate and Nardil, two of the first monoamine oxidase inhibitors (MAOIs), which were the first antidepressants, because aspects of their chemical compound altered the moods of patients suffering from tuberculosis (TB). Monoamine oxidase is an enzyme that blocks the reuptake of some neurotransmitters such as norepinephrine and serotonin and thereby alleviates symptoms of depression. MAOIs are rarely prescribed in the United States because of their many potential side effects. These include: dramatic changes in blood pressure; nausea; dizziness; and, in a small number of patients, dangerous cardiovascular problems. However, doctors still rely on MAOIs as reserve medications, using them to treat otherwise treatment-resistant bipolar depression. In other words, if all other drug options fail, doctors sometimes prescribe MAOIs, although these medications are rarely used when treating children or adolescents.

Patients taking MAOIs should exercise caution. These anti-depressants can have harmful side effects, especially when combined with other drugs. Certain cough syrups, diet pills, decongestants, and asthma medications interact negatively with MAOIs. As a result, an excessive release of the neurotransmitters dopamine, epinephrine, and norepinephrine can severely elevate blood pressure. Some narcotic medication such as morphine, codeine, and Demerol can interact with MAOIs, fatally increasing serotonin levels in the body. The use of MAOIs also requires strict dietary restrictions. Patients should avoid beans, aged cheese, yogurt, alcoholic beverages, preservatives, sausage and pepperoni, soy sauce, certain fruits and vegetables, and tofu. This is not a complete list.

Potentially Serious Side Effects

If even one of the following side effects occurs while taking an MAOI medication, please discontinue its use and immediately call your doctor or emergency services.

☞ Severe headache

☞ Nausea

☞ Uneven heartbeat

☞ Chest pain

☞ Sweating or cold, clammy skin

☞ Dilated pupils

☞ Neck stiffness

☞ Bleeding from the nose

Please ask your doctor to outline the dietary restrictions before you start taking MAOIs.

Some people may feel that America's doctors are over-prescribing drugs, writing out prescriptions of antidepressants such as Prozac for every ailment from job-induced stress to premenstrual syndrome (PMS). However, this is not a forum for the debate of whether or not physicians should be prescribing antidepressants. This book does aim to supply each reader with enough information to question doctors about how drug therapy may impact his or her own case.

This is not to say that antidepressants aren't part of a drug-treatment regimen for bipolar patients. Drug therapy is the most widely used method to return a sense of normalcy to people with mood disorders. Antidepressants do work well in most individuals who are coping with bipolar disorder if a doctor's instructions are followed carefully. This includes remaining on a daily medication regimen, even when the depressive or manic symptoms subside.

Keith

My treatment has been like a roller-coaster ride. It's as if you're a passenger on a ride that has so many ups and downs and you think it will never end. What I eventually realized, though, was that the most important aspect of drug treatment is to remain hopeful. The medications do work. Patience is the key.

Antipsychotics

Bipolar individuals coping with unusually strong manic symptoms may lose touch with reality or may become psychotic. Symptoms of psychosis include hearing voices, feeling paranoid, seeing things, and believing that one is being followed or stalked. Because weeks can pass before mood stabilizers begin to take effect, doctors sometimes prescribe antipsychotic medication to individuals with bipolar disorder. An antipsychotic drug can immediately stop racing thoughts, pressured speech, and the over-activity associated with mania. Doctors prescribe anti-psychotics as needed, sometimes on a short-term basis.

Antipsychotics were developed in the 1930s when scientists began experimenting with a group of chemical compounds called phenothiazines. Many of the compounds had sedative properties and were later discovered to be rather useful during surgical procedures. One drug in this group, chlorpromazine (thorazine) was then used to treat schizophrenic patients. Doctors found that chlorpromazine not only helped calm patients but reduced their hallucinations and delusions.

Today, researchers have developed antipsychotic medications such as clozapine (Clozaril), olanzapine (Zyprexa), quetiapine (Seroquel), risperidone (Risperdal), and ziprasidone (Zeldox). These drugs have the same benefits but have fewer side effects. If you are taking any of these drugs, your doctor may also request frequent blood tests to monitor your dosages.

The side effects of antipsychotic medications can include dry mouth, sleepiness, constipation, and blurred vision. Antipsychotics may also debilitate the body's muscle tone, inhibit movement, and induce tardive dyskinesia (TD)—a repetitive involuntary movement of the facial muscles that causes a person to look as if he or she is chewing, blinking, or sporadically moving his or her lips. TD goes away a short time after a patient stops taking antipsychotic medication.

Other Medications

Doctors may recommend other medications to treat bipolar disorder. Their recommendations often depend on the severity of the patient's symptoms. Some of these drugs are sold over the counter (available without a doctor's prescription). Some seem to have beneficial effects on mild versions of bipolar disorder, specifically on hypomania.

Many patients also leave the doctor's office with a prescription for benzodiazepine, a sedative that combats anxiety and stress. Sometimes, short-term use of an effective drug like benzodiazepine can calm states of mania, especially when used in conjunction with antipsychotic medications. This is a controlled substance and should be utilized with care. It can be psychologically addictive. Withdrawal symptoms may include seizures, so if you or your family have a history of seizure, this is not a drug option for you.

Doctors can also prescribe stimulants to patients suffering from severe bipolar depression, but since the advent of antidepressants in the mid-1980s, they tend to do so less and less. Stimulants such as amphetamines can boost energy levels, as well as increase concentration and elevate mood, but they are also quite addictive. They raise blood pressure and increase the potential for heart problems.

Thyroid medications, or hormone therapy, can also alter the moods of people with bipolar disorder. A normal part of therapy to help bipolar patients is the proper regulation of the thyroid gland. For years, doctors have observed a correlation between hormone levels and mood. For instance, cycles of depression can intensify in a woman just before and during her menstrual cycle when hormones are at their highest monthly level. Other studies indicate that hypothyroidism is very common in bipolar patients who are rapid-cycling. Postpartum depression (the time after a woman gives birth and when increased hormone levels can induce a reactive episode of depression) also has a hormonal link. It is for this reason that doctors test patients for thyroid conditions before beginning any drug treatment for depression.

Patients should be on the lookout for the symptoms of thyroid dysfunction. Abnormally low thyroid functioning, known as hypothyroidism, can cause weight gain and sluggish or slow behavior. Overactive thyroid functioning, or hyperthyroidism, can cause a rapid pulse rate, an increase in nervous energy, feelings of anxiety, tension, and undue stress. Of course, these symptoms are general and blood tests must be completed to properly determine thyroid dysfunction. If one is found to have either hypo- or hyperthyroid problems, medications can be prescribed to boost or lower the body's level of hormones.

St. John's Wort

A natural, yellow-flowering herb, St. John's Wort has exploded in popularity in recent years due to its seemingly positive effects on symptoms of depression. However, it is not necessarily effective for the depressive symptoms of bipolar disorder. Europeans have been using the herb for years and conducting clinical tests to demonstrate its effectiveness as well. One such test, published in the *British Medical Journal*, found that 55 percent of patients with mild to moderate depression claimed that taking the herb improved the quality of their lives.

Researchers are not certain exactly how the herb works, but extensive studies in the United States on St. John's Wort are forthcoming. Scientists believe that the herb works in the same manner as its chemical sibling, Prozac: It naturally slows the breakdown of serotonin and alters other neurotransmitters associated with depression, including dopamine and norepinephrine. Like other antidepressants, several weeks may pass before its effects become noticeable.

A word to the wise, however. St. John's Wort renders birth control pills ineffective in female patients and it should never be taken while in conjunction with anti-depressants. This combination could lead to a rise in blood pressure or to a condition called serotonin syndrome that causes increased sweating, agitation, unusual muscle con-tractions, nausea, and insomnia. More severe cases of sero-tonin syndrome can cause seizures, coma, and even death.

Electroconvulsive Therapy

Cinematic images of electroconvulsive therapy (ECT) are often horrifying: Patients strapped to a bed bite down on rubber mouthpieces while metal plates send pulses of electricity through palpitating limbs. The reality is that, especially for seriously manic or depressed individuals, ECT works quickly and successfully, with very few perma-nent side effects. In fact, in 80 percent of bipolar cases, ECT treatments immediately relieve manic symptoms.

Medical treatments sometimes change radically over time and such is the case with electroconvulsive therapy. Once an overused treatment feared by patients in the 1940s and 1950s, today's ECT treatments are much more controlled and humane. Now, doctors use anaesthetic drugs (similar to the kind administered before surgery) to temporarily put patients to sleep while the sixty-second ECT treatment is administered. Doctors also administer other drugs (neuromuscular blocking agents) to control a patient's muscle spasms. Scientists now know that if they stimulate only half of the brain (either the right or left hemi-sphere), patients will recover more rapidly and will suffer fewer side effects such as memory loss.

After the initial pulse of electricity is administered (in controlled doses and within timed limits), a patient's right or left brain hemisphere sends the body into an induced seizure which lasts roughly forty-five seconds or less. After approximately fifteen minutes, the patient wakes feeling groggy, slightly woozy, or a bit confused. This reaction is normal and disappears within hours after treatment. ECT's long-term side effects, however, seem to center on the brain's memory capacity. About two-thirds of ECT patients have reported some degree of memory loss. Others suffer a similar fate, one that doctors refer to as retrograde amnesia or temporary memory loss.

Doctors still consider ECT treatment one of the best therapies for extreme depression or mania. A patient is a candidate for ECT treatment if he or she is suicidal, severely depressed but unable to take antidepressant drugs, unresponsive to drug treatments, or in a phase of severe and acute (active) mania. ECT is also recommended for pregnant women suffering from bipolar depression, who are unable to risk the side effects of drugs. When ECT treatments are decided upon as a course of treatment, the administration of all antidepressants and mood-stabilizing medications should stop completely.

Medical professionals still do not know exactly how or why ECT treatments work, but they do know that they put a dramatic and immediate stop to severely depressed or manic symptoms in a majority of patients, even those who have threatened suicide. Sometimes changes occur in as little as three to four sessions. Doctors compare ECT to cardiac defibrillation (the act of applying short, strong electrical pulses to the heart), which starts a stopped heart, causing it to pump blood after it has ceased beating. ECT sends electrical pulses to the brain in the same controlled way. Not surprisingly, scientists have noted a similar reaction in the brain: rapid, continuous firing of neurotransmitters. At this point, research continues into ECT treatment and its effects.

Living with
Bipolar Disorder

Living with bipolar disorder involves a great deal of accep-
tance. Because it is an incurable and sometimes progres-
sive mental illness, bipolar individuals often deny that they
need treatment, or they ignore their course of treatment
and the potential side effects of drugs. Probably the best
advice for bipolar patients is to have patience with your
mental illness and the treatment process. Drug treatment
can effectively manage bipolar disorder. Further, continue
to take your medication until you and your doctor decide
to change your treatment. You can have a normal life.

The Road Ahead

Fortunately, the medical field is a growing and dynamic
industry, constantly inventing new and better treatments.
With new drugs comes increased hope. Currently, there
are no fewer than 103 new psychoactive drugs in clinical trials in the United States and in Europe. Scientists
are coming closer and closer to isolating chromosomes
that have known links to mood disorders like bipolar
disorder in genes associated with the X chromosome. All
continue to agree that a family history of mental illness

as well as environmental influences play a significant role in determining one's mental health.

Diet and Nutrition

Diet plays an important role in helping to control the effects of any symptoms of depression. Some believe it is even helpful when coping with the depressive symptoms of bipolar disorder. Although it is not a treatment in and of itself, recent research has demonstrated that modifying one's diet can actually reduce depressive lows. Further, certain foods, depending on the amounts consumed, may increase or decrease levels of certain neurotransmitters responsible for brain activity related to depressive episodes. For instance, as mentioned earlier, craving sweets and certain carbohydrates can be a symptom of SAD. Carbohydrates do affect the levels of neurotransmitters in the brain, but to what extent remains unclear.

Although refined carbohydrates such as foods rich in sugar can can cause an increase in neurotransmitter production, the effect is not lasting. Doctors more often recommend a diet full of complex carbohydrates such as whole grains, cereals, breads, pastas, fruits, and vegetables. These foods seem to increase energy levels as well as alter brain chemistry and mood.

Increasing your intake of certain vitamins, especially B vitamins, should prove useful in easing depressive symptoms. An increase in vitamin B_6 (found in bananas, avocado, chicken, and whole grains) can increase the production of serotonin. Decreases in B_{12} can affect mental health and stability. Additionally, deficient levels of folic acid (commonly found in leafy greens and in orange juice) in one's diet seems to increase the risk of depression and mood dysfunction.

Minerals also play a role in the prevention of depression. Make sure that you are getting adequate amounts of the following: calcium, iron, magnesium, selenium, and zinc. Adding a vitamin supplement to your diet can also help. Be sure to consult your doctor before taking any vitamin or mineral supplements, however, because some drug interactions, even with vitamins and minerals, can be risky.

The Importance of Exercise and Stress Reduction

Individuals coping with mild to moderate depression often find that daily or weekly aerobic exercise eliminates some symptoms. Studies now indicate that twenty to sixty minutes of walking, running, jogging, or dancing—essentially any aerobic exercise—three times per week will have some positive effects on those who suffer from depression, in as little as five weeks. Although exercise may help alleviate depressive symptoms, there is little research that shows its effectiveness in treating the depressive symptoms of bipolar disorder.

Nevertheless, various scientific theories tout the positive effects of increased physical activity. One reason could be the body's increased production of endorphins (neurotransmitters linked to feelings of well-being) during exercise. Like MAOI antidepressants, exercise seems to increase amounts of other neurotransmitters that fight depression. Doctors also support the use of exercise therapy because it is cost-effective, distracts patients from focusing solely on their problems, and can become a form of meditation.

A study of depression conducted at Duke University drew important conclusions about exercise and the repression of depressive symptoms. According to Duke psychologist James Blumenthal, research showed that "the effectiveness of exercise seems to persist over time, and that patients who respond well to exercise and maintain that activity have a much smaller chance of relapsing." The Duke study determined that as levels of exercise increased, so too did one's feeling of well-being. Blumenthal continued, "We found that there was an inverse relationship between exercise and the risk of relapsing. The more one exercised, the less likely that person would see his or her depressive episodes return. For each fifty-minute increment of exercise, there was an accompanying 50 percent reduction in relapse risk." In addition to changes in diet and increased exercise, the following are also ways you can improve your overall mental health.

- **Follow a normal sleep schedule**. Research has shown that an interruption in normal sleep patterns has the potential to trigger manic episodes. Try to go to sleep and wake up around the same time, every day.

- **Do not use alcohol, drugs, or caffeine**. Other than medications, any substance that interferes with the body's natural cycles, or acts as a stimulant or depressant, could trigger manic or depressive episodes.

- **Listen to your body**. Learn to watch for the typical early warning signs of an oncoming manic or depressive episode.

⮑ **Seek support from friends and family**. They are there to help. Communicate calmly and speak clearly about what you are going through.

⮑ **Search for a doctor you can trust**. The doctor-patient relationship plays an integral part in the development of an individualized plan of treatment. Ask questions. Education can help prevent future mood swings.

Support of Family and Friends

A large part of learning to live with bipolar disorder involves learning to depend on emotional support from others. Initially, any diagnosis of mental illness is difficult to absorb. Many individuals go through periods of anger, denial, or even indifference. Initially, the diagnosis may seem like a lifelong ticket to doctors and medications. After the onslaught of evaluations, questions, and doctor visits comes maintenance and, ultimately, stability. A big part of that stability is often derived from family and friends.

Family members need to become knowledgeable about bipolar disorder. They also need to remember that a person diagnosed with an emotional illness such as bipolar disorder does not have control over his or her moods. Unlike people who can exert power over their emotions, people who suffer with mood disorders cannot monitor reactions that may seem inappropriate or unwarranted. They cannot "snap out of it," or "pull themselves together."

Family members should be very careful not to criticize or forget that medications sometimes require time and adjustment to work efficiently. In general, friends and family need to have patience, to speak in clear and uncritical language, and to be objective about their interpretation of symptoms. Supporters needn't blame the illness for every action or statement. Every late-night cramming session is not the beginning of mania, and sleeping in on a Sunday morning is not a telling sign of depression. Communicate as openly and as honestly as possible while understanding that with sustained treatment and support, mood disorders, like most mental illnesses, can be managed.

It is possible to live a happy and productive life if you are bipolar and in treatment. A patient should learn as much as he or she can about the nature of mood disorders and his or her own, as well as family history of the disease. In this way, an individual can come to terms with the disorder, find the right treatment, and live a happier, more productive, and emotionally stable life.

Glossary

anhedonia A psychological condition characterized by inability to experience happiness in normally pleasurable acts.

antidepressants A select grouping of medications that are used to elevate the mood of a person in treatment for depressive illness.

bipolar disorder A mood disorder characterized by mania and depression, sometimes with intervening periods of normal mood.

compulsive Describes an individual who is prone to compulsions, or irresistible impulses, to perform irrational acts.

dementia A mental disorder characterized by defects in memory, judgment, orientation, and emotional behavior.

depression Prolonged sadness characterized by loss of pleasure; lowering of mood; changes in sleep, appetite, and activity level; as well as problems with memory and concentration.

dopamine A neurotransmitter in the central nervous system.

dysthymia A mild depressive state, usually chronic, but not severe enough to be considered clinical depression.

dysthymic disorder A mild to moderate depressive disorder persisting chronically for at least two years.

electroconvulsive therapy A medical procedure that applies brief electrical discharges to the brain to produce a seizure under controlled conditions.

euphoria A mood state of extreme elation often experienced by people during states of mania.

hallucination A false perception caused by abnormal brain function that can affect sight, sound, smell, taste, and touch.

hypersomnia Excessive drowsiness or need for sleep.

hyperthyroidism Overactivity of the thyroid gland resulting in excessive production of the thyroid hormone, usually causing abnormal functioning of the body and/or brain.

hypomania A mild form of mania.

hypothyroidism Underactivity of the thyroid gland resulting in lowered production of the thyroid hormone, usually causing abnormal functioning of the body and/or brain.

insomnia Inability to sleep.

light therapy A treatment for seasonal affective disorder (SAD) utilizing exposure of affected individuals to light; also known as photo therapy.

mania Sustained, abnormal elevation of mood found in bipolar disorder and often associated with poor judgment, paranoia, grandiosity, hyperactivity, insomnia, and occasional hallucinations.

monoamine oxidase inhibitor (MAOI) A medication that blocks the action of the enzyme monoamine oxidase; often used to treat depression.

neurotransmitter Chemical that functions in the nervous system as part of the process that transmits information from one neuron to another.

norepinephrine A monoamine (chemical) that serves as a neurotransmitter in the brain.

obsession A persistent, unwelcome emotion, idea, or impulse that repetitively and insistently forces itself into one's consciousness and that cannot be eliminated by reason.

obsessive-compulsive disorder A psychiatric disorder manifested by the presence of obsessions and compulsions.

psychosis A state of severe brain malfunction associated with delusions and hallucinations; found in severe forms of psychiatric disorders such as schizophrenia, bipolar disorder, dementia, and acute substance abuse.

rapid-cycling A frequency of bipolar mood swings of at least four per year.

remission A medical term for the disappearance of symptoms of illness.

seasonal affective disorder (SAD) A mood disorder with mood swings occurring predictably at certain seasons of the year, usually fall to winter and/or spring.

selective serotonin reuptake inhibitor (SSRI)   A class of antidepressant medications.

serotonin A monoamine that serves as a neurotransmitter in the central nervous system.

synapse The area between the end of one nerve cell and the beginning of another, at which point impulses are transmitted from one cell to the next.

thyroid gland A gland located in the neck in front of the trachea (windpipe) and producing a hormone that regulates body and brain functions.

tricyclic A class of antidepressant medications.

Where to Go for Help

The D/Art Program (Depression/Awareness,
    Recognition, and Treatment)
National Institute of Mental Health
6001 Executive Boulevard, Room 8184
Bethesda, MD 20892-9663
(301) 443-4513
Web site: http://www.nimh.nih.gov

Depression and Related Affective Disorders Association (DRADA)
Meyer 3-181, 550 Building
Johns Hopkins Hospital
600 North Wolfe Street
Baltimore, MD 21287-7381
(410) 955-5800
Web site: http://infonet.welch.jhu.edu/departments/drada/default

The National Alliance for the Mentally Ill (NAMI)
    Colonial Place Three
2107 Wilson Boulevard, Suite 300
Arlington, VA 22201-3042
(800) 950-NAMI (6264)
Web site: http://www.nami.org

The National Alliance for Research on
    Schizophrenia and Depression (NARSAD)
60 Cutter Mill Road
Suite 404
Great Neck, New York 11021
(800) 829-8289
(516) 829-0091
Web site: http://www.mhsource.com/narsad

The National Depressive and Manic-Depressive
Association (DMDA)
730 North Franklin Street
Suite 501
Chicago, IL 60610-7204
(800) 82-NDMDA (63632)
Web site: http://www.ndmda.org

The National Mental Health Association
1021 Prince Street
Alexandria, VA 22314-2971
(800) 969-NMHA (6642)
(703) 684-7722
Web site: http://www.nmha.org

In Canada

Canadian Mental Health Association
2160 Yonge Street, Third Floor
Toronto, ON M4S 2Z3
(416) 484-7750
Web site: http://www.cmha.ca

Mood Disorders Association of British Columbia
2730 Commercial Drive, Suite 201
Vancouver, BC V5N 5P4
(604) 873-0103
Web site: http://www.mdabc.ca

Web Sites/Support Groups

Internet Mental Health
http://www.mentalhealth.com

Pendulum Resources Bipolar Disorders Portal
http://www.pendulum.org

For Further Reading

Arterburn, Stephen. *Hand-Me-Down Genes and Second-Hand Emotions.* New York: Oxford University Press, 1993.

Barondes, Samuel, H. *Mood Genes: Hunting for Origins of Mania and Depression.* New York: Oxford University Press, 1999.

Goodwin, Frederick K., and Kay Redfield Jamison. *Manic Depressive Illness.* New York: Oxford University Press, 1990.

Jamison, Kay Redfield. *An Unquiet Mind: A Memoir of Moods and Madness.* New York: Vintage Books, 1996.

Jamison, Kay Redfield. *Touched with Fire: Manic-Depressive Illness and the Artistic Temperament.* New York: Free Press, 1996.

Klein, Donald F., and Paul H. Wender. *Understanding Depression.* New York: Oxford University Press, 1993.

Kramer, Peter D. *Listening to Prozac.* New York: Penguin Books, 1997.

Mondimore, Francis Mark. *Bipolar Disorder: A Guide for Patients and Families.* Baltimore, MD: Johns Hopkins University Press, 1999.

Mondimore, Francis Mark. *Depression: The Mood Disease.* Rev. ed. Baltimore, MD: Johns Hopkins University Press, 1993.

Morrison, Andrew L. *The Antidepressant Sourcebook: A User's Guide For Patients and Families.* New York: Doubleday, 1999.

Murray, Michael T. *Natural Alternatives to Prozac.* New York: William Morrow and Company, Inc., 1996.

Smith, Jeffery. *Where the Roots Reach for Water: A Personal and Natural History of Melancholia.* New York: North Point Press, 1999.

Styron, William. *Darkness Visible: A Memoir of Madness.* New York: Vintage Books, 1992.

Whybrow, Peter C., M.D. *A Mood Apart: The Thinker's Guide to Emotion and Its Disorders.* New York: Harper Collins Publishers, 1998.

Index

A
aggression, 2, 27
alcoholism, 13, 38
*American Journal of
    Psychiatry*, 37
anhedonia, 29–30
*Archives of General
    Psychiatry*, 31
Areteus, 5

B
Baillarger, Jules, 8
"Bells, The," 11–12
bipolar disorder, subcategories of
    bipolar I, 37–39, 42
    bipolar II, 37–39, 42
    cyclothymic disorder, 37,
        40–41
    rapid-cycling bipolar
        disorder, 37, 41–42, 73
bloodletting, 7
blood pressure, 2, 73
Blumenthal, James, 81
Bonet, Theophile, 8
British Medical Journal, 74

C
Cade, John E., 58–59
chlorpromazine, 9–10
Churchill, Winston, 30
cognitive-behavioral
    therapy, 54
cognitive therapy, 53–54
cyclothymia, 9, 61

D
delusions, 23, 25
depression, 1–3, 6, 8–9, 14–17,
    23, 28–32, 37, 39, 41,
    53–54, 74
    clinical, 2
    reactive, 29
    studies of, 10
    symptoms of, 29–34
    unipolar, 2, 15, 28–29, 39,
        46, 50
diagnosis, 3, 4, 48–50
*Diagnostic and Statistical
    Manual of Mental
    Disorders*, Fourth Edition
    (*DSM-IV*), 17, 26
diet, 4, 79–80
Dickinson, Emily, 11, 30
Drug Price Competition and
    Patent Term Act of
    1984, 68
drug therapies, 4, 9, 10, 48–49,
    51, 55–63, 64–75
    barbiturates, 9
    benzodiazepines, 56, 73
    carbamazepine, 61, 64
    clozapine, 56
    gabapentin, 62
    lamotrigine, 62, 64
    lithium, 4, 38, 41, 48,
        56–59, 60, 61, 64
    narcotics, 9
    Risperdal, 56
    side effects, 57, 58, 59,
        60–61, 62, 63

topiramate, 63
valproate, 60–61

E
electroconvulsive shock therapy,
    20, 56, 75–77
Eliot, T. S., 11, 31
Enlightenment, age of, 8
environment, 3, 10, 39
euphoria, 6, 39
euthanasia, 7
euthymia, 18
exercise, 4, 80–81

F
Falret, Jean-Pierre, 8
Fitzgerald, F. Scott, 13
Food and Drug Administration
    (FDA), 59, 67
Freud, Sigmund, 9–10

G
Galen, 6
genetics, 3, 6, 10, 13–14, 46–47
Gogh, Vincent van, 10
grandiosity, 16

H
hallucinations, 25
Hemingway, Ernest, 13
Hippocrates, 5, 32
homeopathic treatments, 4
hormone levels, 2, 73
hostility, 2, 25
humoralism, 6, 7
humors, 5–6
hypersomnia, 30, 43
hyperthymic temperament, 43
hyperthyroidism, 74
hypomania, 25–27, 32, 38, 72
hypothyroidism, 57, 73, 74

I
irritability, 2, 17, 25, 30

J
James, Robert, 8
Jamison, Kay Redfield, 10, 11,
    13, 31, 34
Johns Hopkins School of
    Medicine, 10
Journal of the American Medical
    Association, 59

K
Kahlbaum, Karl Ludwig, 9
Kerouac, Jack, 13
Kraeplin, Emil, 9, 46
Kramer, Peter D., 67

L
lamotrigine, 62
Lilly, Eli, 68
Listening to Prozac, 67
lobotomy, 9
Lowell, Robert, 13
lunatic, 7

M
mania, 1, 3, 8–9, 16–27, 32, 33,
    37, 39, 41, 49, 54
    black mania, 17
    psychotic mania, 25
    stage I mania, 19, 21–22
    stage II mania, 19, 23–24
    stage III mania, 19, 24–25
    symptoms of, 18–25
    white mania, 17
medications, 27, 48, 50
    antidepressants, 42, 51, 55,
        64–65, 70–71
    antipsychotics, 51, 55, 56,
        64, 71–73

chlorpromazine, 72
clozapine, 72
monoamine oxidase
    inhibitors (MAOIs), 64,
    69–70
mood stabilizers, 48, 51,
    56–63
olanzapine, 72
phenothiazines, 72
Prozac, 67, 68, 70, 74
quetiapine, 72
risperidone, 72
St. John's Wort, 74–75
selective serotonin reuptake
    inhibitors (SSRIs) 64, 67
side effects, 66–73
tricyclics, 64, 66–67
ziprasidone, 72
melancholia, 5–6, 32
Mendel, Emanuel, 26
mood disorders, 13–14, 28, 39,
    44, 46, 50–51
mood swings, 1–3, 13, 32, 39, 49

N
National Depressive and Manic-
    Depressive Association, 4
National Institute of Mental
    Health, 13
neurotransmitters, 31, 44, 45,
    47, 60, 65, 74
    dopamine, 74
    endorphins, 80
    norepinephrine, 74
Night Falls Fast: Understanding
    Suicide, 34

P
paranoia, 25
Petty, Fred, 47

photo therapy, 44
physicians, 5, 8, 13, 51
Plath, Sylvia, 11
Plato, 7
Poe, Edgar Allan, 11–13
Pollack, Jackson, 10
psychiatrists, 3, 16, 19, 20, 29,
    33, 43, 51–53
psychologists, 3, 51–53
psychotherapy, 49, 50
psychotic, 3

R
relapsing and remitting, 4
religion, 7–8, 24, 31
Roethke, Theodore, 11
Rothko, Mark, 10

S
schizophrenia, 46, 50
seasonal affective disorder
    (SAD), 43–44
serotonin, 31, 44, 64, 67, 74
Socrates, 7
spending money impulsively,
    18, 19
Styron, William, 30
substance abuse, 13–14, 18, 39
suicide/suicidal thoughts, 14,
    31, 34–36, 59, 68, 76

T
Textbook of Psychiatry, 9
Thorazine, 9

W
Williams, Tennessee, 13
Woolf, Virginia, 11

About the Author

Joann Jovinelly is an editor and writer who has developed and edited several nationally published magazines. She has also worked as a newspaper reporter and as a music journalist. She lives in New York City.

Acknowledgments

Many thanks to everyone that I interviewed for their personal insights into bipolar disorder; to Kerry P. Callahan, who kindly edited this book; and to Jason, without whose help I would never have come this far.